Connections

Connections

USING PERSONALITY TYPES TO DRAW PARENTS & KIDS CLOSER

JIM BRAWNER

WITH DUNCAN JAENICKE

FOREWORD BY GARY SMALLEY

MOODY PRESS

CHICAGO

To my wife, Suzette,
and
to our children,
Jason, Travis, and Jill:
in this book and in our
marriage we present to you
our lifetime commitment

Contents

Foreword

Every time I read a parenting book, I always secretly wish I could peek in on the author's family to see if he's really living what he writes about. In this case, my wish has come true. In all my travels over the past years and after meeting thousands of families, there's one that stands out right near the top—the Brawner home.

Something I appreciate about Jim and Suzette is that they did not set out to write a helpful parenting book just to have a strong family. But they have succeeded on both counts.

In this book you'll learn how to motivate your children, how to appreciate each child as a unique individual, how to understand their feelings and needs, how to laugh with them, and how to gain encouragement and wisdom for the tough times.

When Jim Brawner gives us advice on parenting, we can take it right to the bank and be assured of receiving high interest on our investment!

GARY SMALLEY

Acknowledgments

I would like to express my deepest thanks to the following people:

To our parents—Buster and Bonnie Brawner, and Fred and Nina Bollen—who have combined for ninety-four years of marriage, a commitment matched by few marriages today.

To my brothers, Jerry and Joe, and to my sister, Janet, who have weathered the storms and enjoyed the sunshine in life with me.

To Priscilla Jaenicke, Duncan's wife, and to their two incredible children, Bethany and Grace. Their humor, wit, and love permeate all who know them and get the chance to cross their paths. The Jaenickes model the "shot in the arm" that the American family needs today. I will be forever grateful to Duncan for helping me with this project.

To Gary Smalley and John Trent, the two best "coaches" I have ever had (not bad, considering that four of my former coaches are or have been head coaches in the NFL). Their encouragement and direction kept this dream alive.

To Jim Watkins for his organizational and communications gifts.

To Spike and Darnell White, who over the past twenty years have been finishing the parenting job that my mom and dad began.

To the entire Kanakuk Kamp family for their love and support.

To the many people who have willingly given their time to the manuscript, especially the following: Jim and Gay Cunningham, Susan Warner, Joe Cross, Cathy Pender, and Sam Nowicki.

CHAPTER ONE

It's a Jungle Out There

It's 5:00 P.M.—feeding time at the Brawner Zoo. Suzette and I herd our three offspring into the minivan and venture forth into the flashing lights of Branson, Missouri's fast-food jungle.

As we make our way down Route 76—home to every burger, chicken, pizza, and ice cream franchise in the known universe—the rumbling of stomachs moves to the vocal chords.

Travis, my fourteen-year-old son, knows exactly what he wants. "Wendy's® is where we're going!" he roars. It's a Dave's Deluxe® burger or nothing for Travis.

My wife—practical by nature—approaches a fast-food safari armed with a fistful of coupons. "Wendy's has a buy-one-get-the-second-one-free sale, so let's be thrifty and go there," she urges.

Ten-year-old Jill and I scan the neon jungle for a packed parking lot.

"Let's just drive down the road and wherever the action is, let's go there!" Jill contributes. If the eating spot has lots of kids, a slide, a roomful of plastic balls to jump into, or a "fun meal," that settles it for my daughter.

Sixteen-year-old Jason waits to hear what other family members want.

"Where would you like to eat, Jason?" is generally answered with, "Whatever makes everyone else happy, I'm willing to go along."

Fortunately Wendy's parking lot is packed because of the buy-one-get-one-free offer on Dave's Deluxes, so all is well with the entire Brawner Zoo—at least momentarily.

Living with so many different types of people does take on the feel—and sound—of a zoo sometimes. Sound familiar?

Our home—and I'd be willing to guess yours too—features a menagerie of different personality types. But that does not mean that families have to take on a "survival of the fittest" mentality.

We'll look at the four basic personality types and discover how each is very different. And we'll learn that each of us is actually a blend of all four traits. With that understanding, each member of the family can allow others to be themselves. I've discovered that major problems can emerge in a family if each person is not understood and cared for as a unique individual.

We'll examine the differences between how males and females act and how that can help each person interact with the opposite sex—whether sibling or parent. And we'll look into how children of different ages view life, and how we can adapt our parenting style to those differences. The number-one teenage complaint and alleged cause of suicide among kids aged thirteen to eighteen is weak relationships at home. I hope this book will be one more tool to help you build strong and supportive family relationships—even if you're a single parent.

Finally, we'll delve into the wide world of communication—both verbal and nonverbal. We'll flesh out that adage "Actions speak louder than words" and find out how to improve our relationships through better communication.

Thus you'll learn how to motivate your children in an honest and effective manner, maximizing family harmony and minimizing family stress and friction. You'll discover how your family can relate to one another more like a wild game preserve than feeding time at the piranha tank!

WORRISOME TRENDS IN THE WILD KINGDOM

Before we get into how to better understand each other, we need to take a step back and look at the landscape. How are families in America faring today? And, more important, how is society affecting our particular family?

Unfortunately, all is not well in American familyland. Oftentimes we indulge in a little self-delusion and either ignore or minimize the bad things that are happening in families today, but that doesn't solve the problems. We need to look bravely at what the environment around us is like so that we can better combat the destructive forces arrayed against us.

My personal "save the family" crusade began one Saturday morning ten years ago as I sat in my favorite restaurant reading the paper. On the front page was an article about Jan, a student from the high school where I coached and taught. Jan was a bright, attractive, "A" student in my tenth grade health class. She had few friends. A loner by choice, I thought.

Just twenty-four hours prior I had stood in my first-hour class as the usual "Friday frenzy" filled the classroom with excitement of the weekend ahead. "Today, we'll go over the last test," I announced. "According to the scores it looks like we need to go over the section on social pressure and how it affects us individually." Jan had aced the test —as usual—but little did I know the topic was not just an academic exercise for her.

Suddenly she burst into tears, bolted from her chair, and dashed from the classroom. As the class sat in stunned silence, my eyes focused on Leanne, one of Jan's few friends.

"Leanne, why don't you check on Jan?" The class silently watched as Leanne left. "OK, class," I continued, trying to pull the class's focus back to the test results. "Let's turn in our books to page seventy-eight." Everyone had a difficult time keeping attention on the test review after Jan's unexplained outburst.

Finally Jan and Leanne returned to the classroom moments before the bell. We watched in silence as Jan's red eyes and smeared mascara testified that something was very wrong. I asked Jan and Leanne to remain after the bell rang.

"Jan," I began, "is there some way I can help?"

She stared at the floor as she wiped away more tears. "It's just some trouble at home. I'll be OK."

"Would you like to talk about it?"

"No. I'll be OK, Mr. Brawner." She got up quickly and hurried to her next class.

That was the last time I ever talked with Jan.

I stared in disbelief at the newspaper headline: "Teen in Critical Condition Following Suicide Attempt." Jan had taken her father's .38 revolver, shoved the barrel into her mouth, and pulled the trigger. After a twelve-hour medical effort to save her life, the fifteen-year-old girl was dead, her life cruelly and irretrievably snuffed out. I was devastated, as were Jan's classmates.

When school resumed on Monday, the loss of a classmate echoed down silent halls and screamed out from the empty chair in each class period. I found it practically impossible to concentrate when my eyes fell on her chair. I wanted to cry.

I learned from Leanne that Jan's parents had filed for divorce, and the final papers had been signed on the Friday that Jan left my classroom. I learned from her other friends that although Jan had not been physically abused, she had been verbally abused. Cuts and bruises heal, but cruel words can cut through children like a bullet.

I've asked myself a thousand times, *How could I have discovered Jan's deep emotional needs early enough to intervene? What could I have done to help her parents affirm her? How can I keep other Jans from ending their lives? How can I help other parents see how powerful—and deadly—unkind words can be?*

Unfortunately, healthy families are rapidly becoming an endangered species. Christian leader and author Dr. Howard Hendricks was asked by a friend of mine recently what can be done to buttress the family.

He sighed heavily. "Despite the flood of Christian seminars, magazine articles, books, and sermons, Christian family life is *still* deteriorating. We're awash in a sea of information, but very little *lasting change* is going on. What we need is not more information, but a way to *integrate* some of that information into our daily lives."

I couldn't agree more. This book is my attempt to introduce practical, field-tested tools that parents and couples can use to improve their relationships. I want to minimize the friction that destroys families and to maximize the harmony God intends for families.

A KEY FLAW: LACK OF INTIMACY IN THE FAMILY CIRCLE

Put one way, at the base of much of the family's troubles lies a problem I call *disconnectedness*; hence the title we have chosen for this book. Moms and dads, sons and daughters are shooting in the dark, groping to reach out and truly understand each other. They want to find an *intimate, warm connection with each other*, but often they lack the tools.

This situation in families today is, sadly, like one popular songwriter puts it in his song "Too Cold at Home." The singer is sitting in a tavern on a hot summer's day, drowning his sorrows in a cold beer. He's not motivated to go home to his wife, either. As he puts it:

> "It's too hot to fish,
> too hot for golf,
> and *too cold at home.*"[1]

Now before you think that such an example doesn't fit many homes, think again. Even if you take away the alcohol from the above scenario, the cold facts remain: *too many families today are merely collections of isolated individuals. They're disconnected from each other, and they desperately need to get connected.*

For example, dads who are struggling to climb the corporate ladder at the office may come home and misguidedly interact with their children and spouses the same way they do with business associates. They sometimes bark orders to wives and children, just like they're the CEO—when God really wants them to be partners with their wives and sacrificial servants to their kids (Ephesians 5:28; 6:4).

And when Dad doesn't get the results he wants, does he switch tools? Does he reconsider his approach? No. He just yells louder. The result is often family carnage, and today we're seeing it in an unprecedented degree.

Yes, family members are groping for each other, and oftentimes they can't even connect with themselves, since they don't understand the whys of their behavior and reaction to certain events or conditions.

The material in this book will hopefully help to bridge that gap in understanding. It can be a large first step toward family harmony; it's working in my family and dozens of other families—and it can in yours.

Robert Young Vs. Bart Simpson

The disintegration of the American family did not start yesterday; it's been gathering steam over the past few decades.

During the fifties, "Beaver" Cleaver never came home to an empty house after school. Latchkey kids were unheard of then. And "grass" was something he whined about having to mow on Saturday morning. Ward, the wise and warm patriarch of the Cleaver family, apparently made enough money that June did not have to work outside the home. Instead she could wear designer dresses and pearls as she made dinner (from scratch—no microwaved suppers for them). Ward's main role, however, was to provide a two-minute moral lesson that neatly resolved any trouble that the Beaver, brother Wally, and "the guys" got into.

Robert Young—who convinced TV audiences between 1953 and 1963 that "Father Knows Best"—reportedly tried to commit suicide after he had been drinking. And Young's cute TV daughter, whom he affectionately referred to as "Kitten," grew up to become addicted to heroin and suffer from psychosis and abject poverty.[2] Thankfully, it seems she has found Christ and has a ministry of evangelism. But such is not always the case; many of the stars who seemed to embody American family life in those early TV years have not found such redemption.[3]

Perhaps you remember the TV show "A Family Affair." It starred Brian Keith as the kindly uncle who adopted his orphaned nephew and niece, Jody and Buffy. Sebastian Cabot played the butler in the Manhattan high-rise; the show ran during the years 1966-71.

I can still picture the little girl, Buffy, with her blond pigtails and her cute smile. She grew up to overdose and die of a combination of cocaine, Quaaludes, and barbiturates at the age of eighteen. The coroner who handled the case in

Oceanside, California, said it was the most lethal drug combination he had ever seen.[4]

Consider the TV families of today, and you'll not be encouraged, either. Bart Simpson has replaced Beaver Cleaver. And Bill Cosby, who portrays Cliff Huxtable, humorously admits that he doesn't know what's best: "Why did [we] have children when all [our] other acts were rational?"[5]

Though the Huxtables are probably the "best" moral family in TV today, even they fall short of the ideal for a Christian family. On a recent episode, the teenage girl was encouraged to abstain from sex with her boyfriend. But what was the rationale? Was it to save herself for her husband? Or at least (and here we're downscaling the moral flavor) to "do the right thing"? How about because of the danger of venereal disease, or even AIDS?

No. It was because "sex is a big step and you shouldn't do it until you've thought about it for a while." Think about that one. Right.

A Gallup survey for *Newsweek* revealed that more than half of us don't know what's best, either. A plurality of those polled thought the family was worse off than just ten years ago. And the future doesn't seem to promise better times: 42 percent of those surveyed felt the family would be worse off ten years from now, the same percentage thought it would be better, and 16 percent weren't sure.[6]

One disturbing trend in our society is the rapid increase of gangs, both in inner-city neighborhoods and even now in the suburbs. Teens don't feel they belong at home—they have no warm, vital connection with their family of origin—so they turn to the gangs for a sense of acceptance, identity, and being heard. Often the price that they pay is drug addiction, jail terms, and too frequently, death. It's frightening to see such a poor substitute for a strong family on the rise.

Further signs of the disintegration of society are not lacking in abundance either:

- An estimated 23,200 people were murdered in the U.S. during 1990, a record-setting pace to date.
- A whopping 29 percent of all Americans were victims of crime in 1988, as compared to Japan, where only 9 percent suffered.
- Living in America's cities seems to be more dangerous than serving in a war: during the Middle East War over Kuwait in 1991, twenty-four Americans died in action; during the time of the war alone, fifty-two people were murdered in Dallas.
- The U.S. has the highest incarceration rate of any nation in the world, with 426 prisoners for every 100,000 citizens.[7]

Why? What has happened in the last thirty years to put the American family on the endangered species list?

Ronald Levant, family researcher at Boston University, believes five forces have contributed to the development of today's family situation:[8] (1) new family planning technologies and practices (giving couples the power to decide if and when to have children); (2) explosion of the divorce rate (with the inception of no-fault divorce); (3) child custody innovations (with blended families and single parent families commonplace and six out of ten children born in the nineties living in a single-parent home before they are eighteen years old.[9]); (4) increase in employment of women; and (5) decrease in the standard of living (for example, salaries not keeping up with housing prices).

MORAL "MEGATRENDS"

Dr. Levant fails to take into account a moral "megatrend" that during the fifties and sixties gave us a humanistic morality, the sexual revolution, and a distrust—if not disrespect—for all authority figures.

Judeo-Christian values had been generally accepted by society at large for most of the past two millennia. Lifelong monogamous relationships between husband and wife, although not practiced by all, were at least the cultural ideal for marriage. God's hatred for divorce (Malachi 2:16) was also shared by society as a whole. Parents, police officers, and government officials were generally respected as "God's servant to do you good" (Romans 13:4).

These moral and ethical shifts away from godly values to humanistic ones in the fifties and sixties were reflected in TV families. The Cleavers were replaced by the Bunkers ("All in the Family"). Archie, unlike Ward, was a cigar-smoking, beer-guzzling couch potato, who hated everyone except Anglo-Saxon Protestants.

His son-in-law, "the meat-head," counterbalanced Archie's ultra-right-wing views with his own liberal campaign for living together, tolerance of homosexuality, civil disobedience, and draft card burning. Not exactly the stuff the Beaver talked about.

The Bunkers have faded into Nielson never-never land, only to be replaced by the domestic disrespect of Al Bundy in "Married . . . With Children" and "Rosanne." These role models of the nineties are no Ozzie Nelson or June Cleaver. For example, Rosanne deals with sibling rivalry by shouting at her two daughters, "All right, you two, fight to the death."

And finally, there is the thermonuclear family called "The Simpsons." Compared to Bart Simpson, the Conner and Bundy kids seem almost respectful and obedient. With one of Bart's favorite phrases being "Eat my shorts," he's no Beaver Cleaver.

Most disturbing, "Rosanne" and "The Simpsons" have been at the top of the ratings. Some family experts explain this success as a reaction to the saccharin-sweet situation comedies of the fifties and sixties. Fathers are not always right. Mothers do not vacuum in designer dresses. Not all children are candidates for Eagle Scouts or are as polite as the Beaver ("Yes, sir." "No, sir.").

But neither are all fathers incompetent, insensitive, insulting losers with an IQ only slightly higher than their belt size. And not all mothers have lousy sex lives, lousy jobs, lousy hairstyles, and even lousier kids. And not all kids are as rude as Bart ("Don't have a cow, man!").

Be Encouraged—You're Their Hero

This book is for families like mine (and probably yours) that fall somewhere between the Cleavers and the Conners. Here you'll learn how to understand these unique and bewildering creatures known as children. I'll share some ideas on motivating your children based on their personality makeup. And you'll discover how to instill your beliefs and values into your children. Most of all, you'll learn how to keep your family off the endangered species list.

Paul Overstreet is a country and western singer/songwriter who turns out hits that are often highly insightful regarding the state of family life today. One of his most inspiring songs, "Heroes," is highly motivating for us parents as we consider this gargantuan task called childrearing. The song serves to remind us of just how our kids view us, especially when we make them a priority in our lives:

> He drives into the city
> And works extra hard all day
> He finishes up early
> So he can get away
> 'Cause there's a blue-eyed kid on second base
> Wants Dad to watch him play
> And Daddy knows he's waiting
> So he hurries on his way
>
> She rocks her crying baby
> In the hours before dawn
> She whispers words of hope to help her husband to
>   hold on

She takes time for the children
Making sure they know she cares
She's more than just a Momma
She's the answer to their prayers

Chorus:

Heroes come in every shape and size,
Making special sacrifices for others in their lives
No one gives them medals
The world don't know their names,
But in someone's eyes they're heroes just the same.

Now I don't pretend to know you
But I bet it's safe to say
There's someone out there somewhere
Looking up to you today
And they see everything you do
Except for your mistakes
You may not think you measure up
But you've got all it takes.[10]

THESE IDEAS WORK

The concepts contained between these covers represent in large part my lifelong goal to help parents understand and motivate their children to a positive outlook on life, to help families be connected instead of disconnected, to help kids flourish instead of die on the vine, and to help parents direct the growth of a healthy family instead of being carried downstream in the floodwaters that carry the wreckage of broken dreams.

I've seen these principles change families in my work as a school principal, a coach, a counselor, and now as the director of a summer camp for young people. I know they can work for you and your "zoo" too. Many families have told me over the years that they've benefited from these concepts.

But the best endorsement and highest motivation for me to write about these principles came from our oldest son, Jason. "You're gonna write a book, Dad? Great! Then everyone can learn how to get along like we do."

A few years ago Gary Smalley and John Trent encouraged me to adapt the concepts they use in describing our basic personality makeup and use them to improve our parenting skills. In the next chapter and those that follow, you'll learn how to better understand yourself, gain greater appreciation for your own and your kids' uniqueness, and increase your effectiveness as a parent.

Notes

1. Bobby L. Harden, "Too Cold at Home." Copyright © 1990 by EMI April Music, Inc. and K-Mark Music. All rights controlled and administered by EMI April Music, Inc. All rights reserved. International Copyright secured. Used by permission.
2. "When Kids Go Down the Tubes: Eight Stories You Won't See on Sitcoms," *People*, March 25, 1991, p. 39.
3. Ibid., p. 38.
4. Ibid.
5. Bill Cosby, *Fatherhood* (New York: Doubleday, 1986), p. 18.
6. "The 21st Century Family," *The Newsweek Poll, Newsweek* special edition, Winter/Spring 1990, p. 18.
7. "The Cities' Deadly Tally," *Newsweek*, March 25, 1991, p. 36.
8. Ronald Levant, *Between Father and Child* (New York: Viking, 1989).
9. George Barna, *The Frog in the Kettle* (Ventura, Calif.: Regal, 1990), p. 66.
10. Paul Overstreet and Claire Cloninger, "Heroes." Copyright © 1990 by Scarlet Moon Music (BMI) (administered by CMI, Nashville, TN) and Juniper Music (ASCAP). All rights reserved. Used by permission.

Thinking It Over

1. When your family heads out to the fast-food jungle, what transpires in your car? Can you begin to make a link between your family members' interaction and the four personality traits? (See "Lions, Otters, Retrievers, and Beavers" in chaper 2.)
2. What are some unique attractions or activities in your area that are conducive to family fun? Of these, which ones do the various family members favor? Why? Do you see a pattern emerging with regard to their preferences?
3. What has changed in our society since the era of "Leave It to Beaver," and how are those changes affecting your family?
4. What family do you know that seems to have it all together? Why do you think they have experienced such success?

CHAPTER TWO

Taming the Family Zoo

Years ago on a trip to the zoo in Little Rock, Arkansas, we saw once again what unique "animals" make up the Brawner menagerie.

As usual, lionhearted Travis had the entire day planned. "First we're gonna see the lions and the tigers, and then we've gotta see the poisonous snake exhibit. That's my favorite!" Simply seeing *some* animals during a nice day at the zoo was not his goal—seeing *all* the animals was. And he was going to direct our movements as well.

By contrast, Jill and I viewed the day as a chance to take in as many exhibits as possible. The fun-loving part of us wanted to be sure to see the monkeys and gorillas.

Jason, who's usually the "whatever makes everyone happy" member of our family, preferred to spend the whole day at the petting pavilion. He would rather make friends with just a few animals than see five hundred animals in one afternoon.

Suzette, who's also a people person, views a trip to the zoo—or anywhere else—as a time to be with the family. She majored on the relational aspects of our outing.

As you can see, there is an incredible variety of personalities in family zoos. And it is important to allow each individual the freedom to roam beyond his preconceived category.

OLD AND NEW ZOOS

Zoos once consisted of concrete buildings made up of long hallways with cages having heavy steel bars on each side. Each exhibit was clearly pigeonholed as to its kingdom, phylum, class, order, family, genus, and species.

There was the wild cat building where lions, tigers, and cheetahs paced back and forth on the cement floor waiting for feeding time. In the primate house, monkeys, chimps, and gorillas climbed bars, swung on tire swings, and snatched up peanuts in their steel and concrete enclosures.

In modern zoos, however, there are few pigeonholes. Animals roam in natural environments. Chimps scamper among imported trees, rocks, and exotic grasses that imitate their native environment. Lions live together in prides and prowl acres of African grasses as visitors ride through their domain in their own cars or "cages" cleverly disguised as safari jeeps on rails.

Franklin Park Zoo in Boston has even solved the problem of northern winters. The revamped zoo features a three-acre domed building with a seventy-five-foot ceiling. Inside the temperature-controlled building, twenty-five species of birds and snakes as well as gorillas, leopards, mandrills, and bongos feel at home among the waterfalls, rocks, cliffs, and foliage.

The family zoo has undergone some dramatic changes in the past thirty years as well. Some trends, as we saw in the previous chapter, haven't been positive. But one positive change is the realization that all children do not neatly fit into one category.

As you have noticed, Jill, Jason, and Travis have three different types of personalities. It's amazing that the same parents in the same environment can produce such variety.

PLACEMAT PERSONALITIES

The Chinese have tried to figure out people for centuries. In their system, all who were born in a certain year are placed in one of twelve categories.

For instance, since I was born in 1951, the placemat in the Chinese restaurant categorizes me (and everyone born in 1963, 1975, and 1987) as a "Rabbit." According to my year of birth, I am "noble and intelligent." See if the following categories describe you.

- Brave and daring Tigers (1950, '62, '74, '86)
- Honest and energetic Dragons (1952, '64, '76, '88)
- Romantic and humorous Snakes (1953, '65, '77, '89)
- Athletic and sophisticated Horses (1954, '66, '78, '90)
- Artistic and pessimistic Rams (1955, '67, '79, '91)
- Humorous and skillful Monkeys (1956, '68, '80, '92)
- Honest but offensive Roosters (1957, '69, '81, '93)
- Nervous and stubborn Dogs (1958, '70, '82, '94)
- Honest but passive Boars (1959, '71, '83, '95)
- Charming and aggressive Rats (1960, '72, '84, '96)
- Quiet and patient Oxen (1961, '73, '85, '97)

It is a colorful system, indeed, but Westerners often have trouble seeing the logic or relationship between such creatures and their characteristics.

FLUID PERSONALITIES

About four hundred years before Christ, Hippocrates, a Greek physician, divided the human race into four temperaments based on a person's balance of four "humors," or body fluids: choleric (choler), melancholy (black bile), phlegmatic (phlegm), and sanguine (blood). Sounds appetizing, huh?

These categories are no longer taken seriously by modern medicine, but the Hippocrates hypothesis did provide some important insights. First, our body's health does affect our outlook on life. For example, doctors are discovering that much depression results from a biochemical deficiency in the nervous system that can be treated with prescription drugs. Second, Hippocrates was correct that certain types of people seem to approach life in a similar manner. (We'll talk more about that in a moment.)

THE MASTER'S MENAGERIE

During the time of the early Christian church, the apostle Paul was aware that there was great diversity in the Master's menagerie. He wrote of them as various parts of the Body of Christ. He affirmed diversity as being a key element for a healthy whole:

> Now the body is not made up of one part but of many. If the foot should say, "Because I am not a hand, I do not belong to the body," it would not for that reason cease to be part of the body. But in fact God has arranged the parts in the body, every one of them, just as he wanted them to be. . . .
>
> The eye cannot say to the hand, "I don't need you!" And the head cannot say to the feet, "I don't need you!" On the contrary, those parts of the body that seem to be weaker are indispensable. . . . If one part suffers, every part suffers with it; if one part is honored, every part rejoices with it. (1 Corinthians 12:14-26)

This passage forever breaks the cookie-cutter concept of Christianity. There are many types of personalities in the Body of Christ. And each one is an important, indispensable individual.

Pastor and speaker Jimmy Johnson writes,

> We have confused holiness with certain temperament or personality traits. Each church has its own standards for a "holy personality." In my denomination, it's the quiet, submissive, morning person who is "holy."
>
> I'm convinced that 90 percent of the problems in churches . . . is not "sin," but trying to force others to conform to our definition of "spiritual" temperaments.[1]

The passage also breaks forever the concept of cookie-cutter parenting. Just as diversity in the Body of Christ is desirable and God-given, so also is diversity in families. Given the wonderful variety of children in our families, it would be ludicrous to raise them all the same way. Yet that's what many parents are trying to do. We'll be spending a major part of this book finding out why parents tend to try to raise all their children the same way and how to correct this approach.

Psychologists cannot agree on how many types of personalities roam this planet. In fact, they can't even agree on how to classify these very different people. Or even what the categories are. For our purposes we're going to define personality as *an individual's characteristic pattern of behavior and thought.*

Each of those words is important. We are unique individuals. There has never been, nor will there ever be, another person who is genetically identical. (Even identical twins have unique fingerprints.) Add to these hereditary differences a variety of experiences, and you have infinitely unique individuals.

Each person has an individual character. That doesn't mean that he will always act in character, but there is an over-all, general pattern for most people's behavior and thought.

Personality, then, is not who we are, but how we act (and react) in most situations.

Family harmony—and strife—occur when these very different kinds of personalities begin rubbing against each other. Sparks can fly, as any parent knows.

Before we begin talking about various types of person-alities, I strongly suggest that you take time right now to have each member of your family fill out one of the follow-ing surveys. You may want to photocopy more surveys so that there are enough for all the members of your family.

After you have filled in the adult or child survey, plot the results on the graph. Take the number of words or sen-tences you circled and make a bar chart in each category. For example, if you circled three words for list L, make a dot on the L scale three points high (see left-hand values). Then connect the dots between the four scales to make a graph. We'll discuss the meaning of the graph later on. (Again, don't skip this step; if you have not taken the test, stop and do so now.)

As we describe various personality types, keep in mind that no type is right or wrong, better or worse. They're just different. The categories simply describe the characteristic ways we think and respond to situations.

Also, be aware that no one is a 100 percent purebred. We are all various mixes of personality types.

Lions, Otters, Retrievers, and Beavers

Let's take a sneak preview of the four types of personal-ity we'll be using in this book: the Lion, the Otter, the Gold-en Retriever, and the Beaver. (But let me urge you to take the test first, before reading the following material. Other-

Personality Survey for Adults[2]

Choose those words or phrases that describe you.

List L

Assertive
Competitive
Decisive
Adventurous
Goal driven

List O

Fun-loving
Motivator
Avoids details
Optimistic
Enjoys change

List R

Loyal
Deep relationships
Avoids conflict
Adaptable
Dislikes change

List B

Orderly
Predictable
Precise, factual
Discerning, analytical
Persistent

Total the number of words circled in each list:

L: _____   O: _____   R: _____   B: _____

Personality Survey for Children

Choose the sentences that are most like you.

List L

I like being the leader.
I say what I think.
I don't like a lot of rules.
I hate to lose games.
I'm not often scared.

List O

I'm funny and playful.
Others like my ideas.
My room is often messy.
I know lots of people.
I like to talk to people.

List R

I have a few close friends.
I'm loyal to my friends.
I want to please others.
I'm kind to others.
I don't like big changes.

List B

I like to do things right.
My room is often neat.
I often hide my feelings.
I'm not good enough.
I do well at school.

Write below the number of sentences you circled in each list:

L: _____   O: _____   R: _____   B: _____

Summary Graph of Results

—— L —— O —— R —— B ——

5

4

3

2

1

0

Name _____   When taken_____

wise you'll be prejudiced from reading the material below.) To illustrate the four personality types, consider this amusing anecdote.

If all four personality types fell off the Empire State Building, they would all experience the same event. But because of their unique personalities, they would have four unique reactions.

The Lion would say, "We're all as good as dead!" (Lions want to get to the bottom line—literally in this case!)

The Beaver would calculate, "We'll all be dead in thirty seconds." (Beavers like precision and planning.)

The Golden Retriever wouldn't say anything but would be looking for a paw to hold. (Togetherness and relationships are more important than outcomes to Retrievers.)

And the Otter would observe, "So far, so good!" (Otters are eternal optimists!)

A POINT OF REFERENCE: OTHER SYSTEMS

The animal-based system used in this book is not the only personality typing system around; there are others. Some of the more popular and widely used ones are the Myers-Briggs Type Indicator, the Taylor-Johnson Temperament Analysis, the Minnesota Multiphasic Personality Inventory (MMPI), Birth-Order concepts, and the Personal Profile System (DiSC). (See the appendix for a discussion of the first four.)

So there are other valid ways of looking at and organizing our behavior. But I've found the system used here—based on the Lion/Otter/Golden Retriever/Beaver criteria—to be the best, especially in terms of reliability, comprehensiveness and ease of understanding.

It was developed by my friend John Trent, based partially on the Personal Profile System (DiSC), by Performax.[3] Trent examined that test, plus thirty others, in an attempt to formulate a user-friendly yet highly reliable personality assessment tool. He and his partner Gary Smalley have done an outstanding job in developing the tool, and I am grateful to them for their input.

INTERPRETING YOUR RESULTS

Now let's interpret the survey you and your family members filled out. Your test will probably have words circled in each of the categories. Most who take this personality test find that they score high on one or two categories and low on one or two categories. And in most cases there is one type that is more dominant than the others.

The most important chart is the bar chart where you plotted the strength of each trait. It graphically reveals the fact that none of us is purely any one type—we're all blends of the four traits. Nevertheless, you'll probably have one or two scales that are higher than the others.

The ideal is to have a healthy balance of all four animals/ traits. (For instance, Suzette's graph is fairly level horizontally because she shows strengths in each personality. Jesus' graph would be the maximum on all four scales, since He was the perfect human during His thirty-three years on earth. Obviously no one human could ever match that.)

As you look over your results, keep in mind that our goal is not to neatly classify—as the older zoos did—but to gain a general understanding of ourselves and the other personalities that make up our unique family zoo.

The principles in this book will help you understand how you relate to others and how others relate to you. And by knowing this, you'll be better able to understand your family and better motivate your children.

L IS FOR LION

As we picture the king of the jungle in our minds, we see one who boldly takes charge and is assertive and determined. Those with pure Lion personalities are goal driven and enjoy difficult challenges. They climb Mount Everest "because it is there"—and are always looking for a goal to achieve.

Our second-born, Travis, is the Lion of our family. You can usually spot a strong Lion without a personality test. He or she has a strong opinion on every subject. (Remember Travis's reactions as we searched for a fast-food restaurant at the beginning of chapter 1? He made clear that it was Wendy's or nowhere.)

If the neighborhood children are playing school, the Lion is the principal. If the children are playing backyard baseball, he appoints himself the captain.

We parents are also a combination of personality types. So as we discuss the various animals, be aware that your personality mix also plays a large role in the makeup of your menagerie. For instance, if both child and parent are Lions, there is a tendency to come at each other with fangs bared. In fact, Lions actually gain energy from confrontations— whereas Golden Retrievers run for cover.

But we'll talk more specifically about understanding and motivating Lions—and the other personality types—in later chapters. We'll cover in depth what motivates and discourages this type, along with their strengths and weaknesses.

O IS FOR OTTER

Those who score high on the O category are extremely verbal and group-oriented. The Otter personality, like its furry counterpart, is fun-loving, energetic, and impulsive. They're great talkers and motivators but hate details and are often shortsighted.

Our third-born, Jill—and her dad—are Otters. (I'm sort of half Otter and half Golden Retriever.) You can easily spot an Otter's room. The bed—if made at all—is just thrown together. The floor is cluttered with half-finished puzzles, partially colored pictures, and two-thirds of a LEGO® project.

Otters love starting things but often get distracted by new opportunities before the original project is completed.

One important—and possibly lifesaving—bit of advice: Never, never, never open an Otter's closet. Jill's idea of cleaning her room is to stuff everything into her closet. You open her closet door at your own risk!

A parent who is purebred Otter will have a good time with his or her children but will run into problems if that trait is allowed to run wild. We'll discuss that more fully in chapter 5.

R IS FOR RETRIEVER

Golden Retrievers are the most loyal. They're tolerant, sympathetic, and easygoing. They're "man's best friend" because they're motivated by relationships and the approval of others. However, they're extremely eager to please, so decision making is difficult, since they don't want to offend anyone.

Our first-born, Jason, is our Golden Retriever. (Remember, he was the one who often answers, "Whatever makes everyone else happy.")

Retrievers' walls are covered with pictures of their friends and posters of their heros. Retrievers are almost the purest form of "people people."

Unless they have some Lion blood, Retrievers can be pushovers as parents. They tend to cave in to children's demands because they want so badly to keep everyone happy.

My wife, Suzette, is a strong Retriever, but she is a balanced blend of Lion, Otter, and Beaver. That allows her to be a peacemaker for our family zoo.

B IS FOR BEAVER

Unlike the let's-have-a-good-time Otter, Beavers work slowly and methodically, with great attention to detail. "Quality is job one" to the industrious Beaver.

Their beds have hospital corners, their closets are arranged in alphabetical order (blouses to vests), and if they're old enough to write, there is sure to be a "to do" list prominently displayed. They are highly analytical, which can be both a strength and a weakness, depending on the situation.

Beavers have something in common with Lions. Both types can be the most insensitive of the parenting animals when pushed to an extreme. A Beaver parent can be too demanding and harsh, literally destroying the self-esteem of his or her offspring. A Beaver's children may attempt to escape the overly rigid atmosphere with drugs, alcohol, or compulsive behavior such as anorexia or bulimia. Similarly, Lion parents, if untempered, can blast their children's self-concept to dust.

BIBLE ANIMALS

I'm often asked after a presentation of these four personality types, "What personality type was Jesus?" The answer is simple: "All of the above." He had the most amazing personality ever, as we noted earlier.

For instance, we see the Lion side of Christ when He roared into the Temple and sent the moneychangers scurrying out of His Father's house (Matthew 21:12-16). He obviously was an Otter who was invited to parties (John 2:2-11) and told entertaining yet convicting parables (Matthew 13:1-52). His Retriever side is seen in His compassion for the crowds and His tears at the tomb of His friend Lazarus (John 11:1-44). Finally, His Beaver side is seen in His careful organization at the feeding of the five thousand: He divided the crowd into groups for distribution and even organized an efficient cleanup committee (Matthew 14:13-21).

Jesus was able to respond appropriately to each type of audience and situation. Just as He was fully God and fully

Man, He was the perfect blend of positive Lion, Otter, Retriever, and Beaver qualities.

"Jesus had the only perfect personality! And that is why all of us are needed to accurately reflect [the body of] Jesus. The strengths of my temperament will offset your weaknesses. Where I am weak, others are strong."[4]

The purpose of examining the four personality types is not so that we can justify our imperfect behavior. "Hey, I'm a Lion; I can't help it if I prowl around growling and snarling at people!" Rather, we want to discover our areas of weakness so that we can allow Christ to mold us closer and closer to His image.

I've noticed that as people allow Christ to work in their lives, they begin to become more balanced in their personalities—closer to the ideal balanced pattern that He would desire.

The book of 2 Peter reminds us of God's desire for us to be balanced. Try to pick out the family animal types in this section of Scripture:

> His divine power has given us everything we need for life and godliness through our knowledge of him who called us by his own glory and goodness. Through these he has given us his very great and precious promises, so that through them *you may participate in the divine nature and escape the corruption in the world* caused by evil desires.
>
> For this very reason, make every effort to add to your faith *goodness;* and to goodness, *knowledge;* and to knowledge, *self-control;* and to self-control, *perseverance;* and to perseverance, *godliness;* and to godliness, *brotherly kindness;* to brotherly kindness, *love.* For if you possess these qualities in increasing measure, they will keep you from being ineffective and unproductive. (2 Peter 1:3-8; italics added)

Did you notice some of our animals in those verses? Lions excel in *perseverance.* Golden Retrievers pulsate with *brotherly kindness* and *love.* Beavers are unsurpassed when it comes to *self-control.*

But we certainly can't allow ourselves to rationalize, "I'm an Otter, so I shouldn't be expected to show self-control." God's plan is that we develop in all areas through our interaction with Him and His children. As we'll discover later, God can use trials and tribulations to moderate some of our too-strong personality traits.

For instance, when I took a personality test ten years ago, I scored as a very high Otter and a very low Lion. I thought, *Lord, help! Here I am going to be a principal and school administrator, and I'm not much of a Lion. I'm in trouble!*

So I've worked on that area. Through various life experiences and specific practice in this area, God has helped develop my Lion scale, to where today I can hold my ground when the situation demands it.

So don't think that your current score will be your profile forever; remember that personality tests are simply a freeze frame or snapshot of one's behavior pattern at that particular point in time. God has designed us to continue growing and changing to be more balanced. It's a lifelong process, and your score will change to reflect your personal growth as the years roll by.

ADAPTING OUR INTERACTION WITH OTHERS

Because Christ has the perfect blend of temperaments, He can relate to each of us right where we are in that lifelong process.

He did so with the disciples: to Otterish/impulsive Peter, Christ was direct and to the point (showing the Lion trait) when He upbraided him over a suggestion that wouldn't fit with God's plan: "Get behind Me, Satan! You are a stumbling block to Me; for you are not setting your mind on

God's interests, but man's'' (Matthew 16:23; NASB*). How's that for being to the point? Wow!

Of course, the classic Lionhearted act on Jesus' part was the clearing of the moneychangers from the Temple (Matthew 21:12-16). He didn't lack for bold resolve when action was called for.

When the Beaver-like Pharisees wanted the woman caught in adultery stoned ("In the Law Moses commanded us to stone such women."), Jesus bared His Lion teeth and calmly said, "If any one of you is without sin, let him be the first to throw a stone at her" (John 8:3-11).

Jesus showed His Otter side when He went fishing (and even walking on the water) with Peter the Otter (Luke 5:1-11; Matthew 14:22-36).

In the case of John the Retriever, He put His arm around the beloved disciple at the Last Supper (John 13:23-25).

Similarly, Christ delegated the Passover details to Peter and John, who must have had the organizational skills of the Beaver. And He often organized large events very well in Beaver-like fashion, as during the feeding of the five thousand. He adapted His interactions with others according to the needs of each individual situation.

In the same way, we parents need to respond to our children in an appropriate way based on their individual temperaments. Like the modern zoo, we must not cage them with our expectations but give them the freedom to become the unique individuals that God created them to be.

Now that we've had a brief orientation to the four-animal system of personality traits, and you've had a chance to see where you and your kids score on the various scales, let's get right into it. As you read about the Lion trait in the next chapter, give some thought as to who around you is strongly endowed with this attribute. It will give you new insight into the behavior of your spouse, your kids, your

*New American Standard Bible.

parents, coworkers and a host of other people in your life—not the least of which is you!

Notes

1. Jimmy Johnson and James Watkins, *Perfect Love* (Indianapolis: Wesley, 1987), p. 50.
2. This test and the four-animal concept in general are adapted from Gary Smalley and John Trent, *The Two Sides of Love* (Pomona, Calif.: Focus on the Family, 1990), p. 35.
3. Another view of the Performax system (especially the biblical aspect) is found in (both book and workbook) *Understanding How Others Misunderstand You* (Chicago: Moody, 1990), by Ken Voges and Ron Braund.
4. Johnson and Watkins, p. 52.

Thinking It Over

1. What personality traits, whether obvious or subtle, become evident when you are on a family outing? Try to name at least one trait for each member of the family.
2. How does each person in your family respond when under pressure?
3. What was the root cause of the last parent/child conflict you experienced? Can you think of a way it could be handled better next time, especially in light of the personality types?
4. On a scale of one to ten (where one represents no conflict and ten represents constant conflict), how is your relationship with each of your children? With your spouse?

CHAPTER THREE

Connecting with the Lion

A hospital call button is a dangerous weapon in the hands of a Lion. When Travis was in the hospital with double pneumonia he had the nurses constantly on the run.

"Get me a 7-Up®!"

"Fluff my pillow."

"When do I get to go home?" (I'm sure the entire staff prayed it would be soon.)

Lions are not patient patients. They want to be in charge of everything—including pneumonia! They say to themselves, *I'm gonna get over this, get out of this bed, and walk out of here.*

And things did not get any better when Travis came home from the hospital.

"Dad, Travis is just sittin' up there tellin' people what to do," my Retriever son Jason complained. "He doesn't say please or thank you or anything. He just says, 'Get it for me!'" I tried to help Jason understand that his brother was born a Lion. And that's not something bad. For instance, it appears that the apostle Paul was a Lion. He wasn't afraid to say what he thought at the early church councils or when face-to-face with Roman rulers. And he wasn't afraid to speak of his faith to some tough crowds.

Without Lionish determination, Paul would have probably called it quits after the first beating or night in jail. Instead, guards who were shackled to Paul must have wondered, *Who's chained to whom?* God was able to use Paul's inborn qualities to do mighty things for Him. In the same way (apart from being rude to nurses), God is helping Travis direct his Lionheart after God's own heart. What a combination!

BORN FREE

During the sixties a movie featuring lions in the wild made the rounds of the nation's theaters. Its theme song, "Born Free," was perfectly suited for the king of the beasts (and Lion children): they freely roam wherever they please, enjoying their kingship to the fullest.

As we've pointed out, there are no good or bad personality types. Some are just more of a challenge to parents. Such are the Lions. This inbred love of freedom is not a sign of rebellion but a result of genetic and environmental background.

Travis's growling and snarling in the hospital was the result of the Lion in him being caged by the illness that put him there.

But it is not just confining physical situations that make Lions pace. Rules, curfews, restrictions—even parents themselves—can give the Lion a case of claustrophobia. Lion kids can be a handful for parents to handle—the key is to recognize when to assert your parental authority. Confrontation is more frequently necessary with such kids than with other personality types.

The secret, then, is understanding the Lion cub and then directing the prowling and growling in the right direction. We'll talk about just how to accomplish that in a few pages, but for now let's continue looking at Lion characteristics.

HOW EARLY CAN YOU SPOT A LION?

John Trent recently told me about a friend's daughter's first day at kindergarten. She came home from school, slammed the door shut, threw her lunch box on the floor, and glared at her father.

Her father, astonished, asked her what the problem was.

"I'm never going back to that school again!" she exclaimed.

"Why not?" inquired her dad.

"Because that teacher didn't do one thing I told her to do!" spit out the five-year-old Lioness. It doesn't take long to spot strong personality traits like this one.

KING OF THE JUNGLE

Lions not only need freedom, they also crave authority like fresh-killed meat. That's why the Travises of the family zoos are always "just sittin' up there tellin' people what to do." This can occasionally get out of hand, but it's a good character quality when tempered correctly.

Travis's soccer coach capitalized on that leadership quality and made him center midfielder. In that position, Travis functions as a field coach. That's not been without problems, as we saw at the outset of this chapter, but it does allow Travis's Lion characteristics to be directed in a positive direction.

It's the heart of a Lion that makes great business executives, coaches, editors, and political leaders (or dictators). And it's also why Lions are such a challenge to parents.

LIONS RISE TO THE CHALLENGE

Another Lion characteristic is the need for a variety of difficult challenges. For instance, one day several years ago Travis, Jason, and their friend Jared were playing with their GI-Joe® figures in the hot tub.

GI-Joe was battling evil forces in the churning water, when suddenly America's hero was blown out of the water and fell unconscious behind—gasp!—the Jacuzzi.

The battle stopped as the three boys stared down the narrow crack between the hot tub and the wall.

"He's gone! GI-Joe is a goner!" Jared wailed.

"Hey, have no fear! I can rescue him," Travis announced with all the authority of a five-star general.

"I don't think you can," Jason responded. "There's not even room to get a broom handle or anything in there."

"Come on, Travis, you can do it," Jared pleaded. "You've gotta save GI-Joe."

Travis climbed out of the hot tub, went into his room, and came back with a flashlight and fishing pole. Within thirty seconds, Travis had made the daring rescue and saved GI-Joe from death among the dustballs. While challenges may frustrate—or even immobilize—other personality types, Lions eat problems for breakfast. They love to rise to the occasion and come through with flying colors.

But it is also this love of challenges that can make Lion kids occasionally whine, "I'm bored." Travis had gone through summer camp, fall football, and winter and spring basketball. The very day after basketball was over, he had been home from school only one hour when he roared, "I'm bored!"

"Can't you just relax, Travis?" I asked more as a rhetorical question. (Lions can't!)

Fortunately the next day the soccer coach called.

"All right, Dad! Now I can go out for soccer!" Travis yelled. Lion blood was once again throbbing through his fourteen-year-old veins. Lions love—and indeed *need*—an almost constant source of challenges and goals.

CHARGE!

Finally, lions are hungry for advancement. Because they are the take-charge type, they love achieving goals and overcoming obstacles. But unlike the Beaver, they aren't as interested in perfection as they are in performance.

Travis has little patience with his Retriever brother Jason and his Otter sister Jill—especially at family meetings. We try to set goals as a family (which is a very Lionish thing to do), but Travis growls and snarls when our family meetings tend toward silliness.

"Come on, let's get on with it. Let's either do something or call this meeting adjourned!" Patience is a skill that we must help our Lion kids to learn (and sometimes us Lion parents, too).

THE COWARDLY LION

Like the famous lion from *The Wizard of Oz*, though, most kings of the jungle are also plagued with fear. Watch children playing table games or sports. Who's the most competitive? The worst loser? Right—Lions!

Lions' greatest fear is to be outperformed. That's why they're so incredibly competitive and insensitive. They have to be the captain, the first in line, the valedictorian, the CEO, chairman of the church board, and so on. Lee Iacocca and Saddam Hussein are typical of this personality type—for good and bad.

I tried to explain this to Jason, our Retriever-hearted son, as it pertained to his brother's in-hospital behavior.

"Travis doesn't realize he's being insensitive, Jason. We have to help him see that."

Whereas Lions may see themselves as decisive and independent, others may see them as harsh and pushy. They may view themselves as determined and efficient, but everyone else may judge them as tough and dominating.

I continued, "But I think God is using this time in the hospital to help Travis. For instance, of all the people in this family, who has had the most problems and traumas in his life?"

"Travis," Jason was quick to answer.

"Why do you think God has allowed all these accidents and illnesses to happen in his life? Because Travis is a Lion, and God wants to make him more sensitive to others."

I shared with Jason—and with Travis—some of my favorite verses, found in James 1:2-4:

> Consider it pure joy, my brothers, whenever you face trials of many kinds, because you know that the testing of your faith develops perseverance. Perseverance must finish its work so that you may be mature and complete, not lacking anything.

Through Travis's trials and testing he has become more sensitive to others and roars a bit less. For instance, he surprised us all when he bought Jill a balloon and candy for Valentine's Day. (His Golden Retriever brother felt so upstaged that he gave Jill some of the candy from his girlfriend's present!)

Remember, practically no one is a 100 percent purebred—we're all a mongrel-style mixture of personalities. It's God's design that we bring our personalities into a balance. That's what being Christlike is all about, since—as we said in chapter 2—He had the perfect personality blend.

Lions also need to understand that even the proud Lion needs a "pride." When Travis was confined to bed he was forced to depend on other people—and on God.

And hopefully he's learning that even Lions need some controls and restrictions. At the modern zoo there are still boundaries and parameters—for the safety not only of humans, but the animals as well.

We are often quick to quote Ephesians 6:1-3:

> Children, obey your parents in the Lord, for this is right. "Honor your father and mother"—which is the first commandment with a promise—"that it may go well with you and that you may enjoy long life on earth."

But it's equally important to obey verse 4, and explain why our parental boundaries are for the child's good: "Fathers, do not exasperate your children; instead, bring them up in the training and instruction of the Lord."

Past experience has helped me discover that if the parameters are reasonable and explained to the child, he or she can still have a blast within the secure and safe environment of those boundaries.

MOTIVATING THE LION

Unlike the loyal Golden Retriever, Lions don't need a lot of "warm fuzzies" and small talk to motivate them. The king of the jungle is goal oriented. He needs clear, specific, brief instructions. "Get to the bottom line!" they often roar.

Because Lions are so achievement oriented, charts are excellent motivators for Lion kids. A check-off chart might include various tasks:

☐ Make bed each morning.
☐ Feed the cat before dark.
☐ Share your toys.

Charts are individual records of accomplishment—which suits this personality type very well. Lions are solitary creatures who don't always participate well in team sports—unless they can be the quarterback or forward (the glory positions). They don't like to share the limelight—or gold stars—with others.

Lions by nature also need a long leash. Because they crave freedom, they prefer choices. This is particularly hard on parents if the first child has been a Retriever or Beaver who needs and wants a very structured environment and specific instructions. But after enjoying a compliant child, suddenly the parent is staring into the jaws of a strong-willed Lion.[1]

One way to meet the Lion's need for a long leash is to give him the freedom to choose when he will do something. Whereas a Golden Retriever wants to know the exact time to feed the cat, a Lion prefers instructions such as, "You must feed the cat anytime before bedtime—you pick the time."

Another technique is to provide a challenge with each task. (Remember, Lions love overcoming obstacles.) For instance, I needed to motivate Travis to rake leaves. Not much of a challenge for a Lion. But our pickup truck was right where I wanted Travis to burn the leaves. What could be a better motivation for a fourteen-year-old Lion than to drive Dad's truck?

Travis attacked the leaves with all the enthusiasm and aggression that a Lion can unleash. You would have thought I promised to let him to drive two hundred miles to St. Louis, rather than just twelve feet. But Travis saw it as a real challenge. A young Beaver, on the other hand, would be absolutely terrified at the prospect of driving my truck. "I don't have a driver's license." "What if I can't stop it?" Not a Lion!

Because Lions love challenges, routine tasks usually cause the child to roar, "That's boring!" But Lions need to learn that some chores—no matter how boring—have to be done. Help your children to create their own challenge for completing tasks, especially routine but necessary ones.

When his children were younger, my friend Jay Norman used to let them play "Double-Dare" when work needed to be done around the house. The popular kid's show features physical challenges that must be done in two minutes or less. But instead of the gooey, messy TV stunts, his children would race the clock to pick up toys in the living room, sweep the front porch, or do whatever needed to be done.

Now that they're older—and chores need to be done instead of watching a video, Jay will push the pause button. The VCR will shut itself off if left on "pause" for more than five minutes, so his kids, Nicole and James, try to beat the timer and get back to their video.

Finally, Lions are strong-willed by nature. And when you have to stare one down, you need to have plenty of ammunition ready. Appeal to their goal orientation and show the positive or negative results if something is done or not done. Instead of just ordering them to "cease and desist" on the basis of your parental authority (which would almost surely provoke a struggle, since Lions tend to fear no one), try saying, "Travis, I can't let you do that. It's dangerous and could hurt others." That usually works out better than simply ordering them about.

And most important, attack the problem, not the person. Lions are hardest on themselves. You rarely have to tell a Lion he has blown it, but parents do need to help the cub see each situation as a learning or disciplining tool for the next challenge. Though Lions are the quickest of the four animals to bounce back, sometimes it takes a little coaxing to bring them out of it.

In such situations, our friend Norma Smalley tries to find the good in the worst situations; she calls it "treasure hunting." That is, in the face of a personal failure or shortcoming, help the child find some lesson to be learned or other good thing to gain from the bad situation. She looks for that silver lining in each dark cloud. Try this technique with discouraged Lion cubs—or any personality type, for that matter.

BEWARE OF TWO LIONS STARTING WORLD WAR III

Since families are dynamic, interconnected organisms, Lion parents need to beware of what can happen when they overreact with Lion children. Though Lion kids are tough, their spirits can be broken just as a Golden Retriever's. After all, they're just kids, not drill sergeants.

A family we're close to, the Jacobys, found that out the hard way, and not a moment too soon. Their eldest daughter, Beth, has a strong Lion trait, as does their father, Dave. Before they learned about personality types, they were frequently clashing when it came to family decision making. Dave was puzzled as to why Beth would constantly challenge his authority when it came to any crossroads where a decision had to be made.

For example, one Saturday in October the family had planned on going to get a pumpkin. Know the feeling? The air is crisp, the leaves are turning, and the ritual of fall has taken hold with a firm grip. Kids are dreaming of the candy they'll get on Halloween night.

Dave proposed they simply go down to the local grocery store and grab some pumpkins. In his Lionish way, he was calculating how time-efficient that would be: *Let's see— we can knock this item off the to-do list in about fifteen minutes, and then I can get to balancing the checkbook, raking the leaves, and washing the car.* He was anxious to maximize that Saturday for to-do's, as he was used to doing during the week at the office.

But Beth had other ideas. "Hey, Daddy, I think we should go look over those fields of pumpkins we saw when we took you to the airport a few weeks ago," she enthusiastically said. "We could get some great pumpkins there! We wouldn't have to get those grungy pumpkins at the store that way!"

Dave just gave her a withering stare. He was interpreting her remarks as "rocking the boat" and challenging his plan.

Beth's countenance fell as her feelings were hurt by the mean look from Dad.

So went the war—at least in the early days of the conflict.

But, thanks to the entrance of four fuzzy creatures into both their thinking, today things are much improved.

Now the Jacobys can look back on those stormy days and through the lens of personality types analyze their misunderstandings. Dave's Lionhearted approach was to take the bull by the horns and make a quick assessment of the situation and then put forth a firm and authoritative decision. In his Lionish way, he would present it as the obvious (and the only) choice. But when his nine-year-old daughter would then put forth her "better idea," he thought she was challenging his leadership in the family. *After all*, he reasoned, *wasn't the biblical concept of headship firm ground to stand on?* (Lion dads don't like to be questioned—they like to be obeyed.)

Yet he soon began to see Beth's "rebellion" was simply normal Lionish behavior. When the two understood each other's personality makeup, their withering stares soon turned to understanding smiles. They began to see both a father and a daughter with strong leadership gifts, and they stopped chafing at each other. They started to work together to find the best decision at each crossroad.

Dave stopped doing what the Bible warns us not to do—namely, provoking our children to wrath (Ephesians 6:4)—and started enjoying his daughter's gifts. What had start-

Lions at a Glance

Lions tend to like:
> Freedom
>
> Leadership roles
>
> Competition, challenges
>
> Goals
>
> Reasons for doing things

Lions tend to fear:
> Coming in second—in anything.

Lions are motivated by:
> Goals, individual achievements
>
> Directions, not demands
>
> Freedom to make choices
>
> Challenges

ed out as a destructive relationship pattern became a blessing.

Today Dave says with a sigh of relief, "I shudder to think how our relationship could have ended up if we had continued our clashes much beyond age nine! Today Beth and I have a newfound joy and respect in our relationship due to this awareness."

Dave's wife, Penny, also testifies with relief, "I was really worried when I saw them frequently arguing, but I didn't know how to approach it, since I didn't understand the dynamics. Now I have some 'handles' to hang our interactions on. It's a tremendous comfort to know that their relationship isn't headed toward disaster anymore."

Next we look at the fun-loving Otter. For those of you who have either a mate or child with this predominant characteristic, you'll find new understanding for why they act the way they do. (This will be especially helpful if you have strong Beaver traits.)

We'll look at how they view life, why they have trouble being serious, why they are constantly distracted, and why Otter kids hate to do chores (not to mention Otter parents). This usually delightful personality trait can sometimes get out of hand, and we'll look at how you can most effectively parent kids blessed with this orientation.

Note

1. Dr. James Dobson on his radio show often uses the phrase "strong-willed" child for the Lion that we're describing. In contrast, his "compliant" description would fit the Golden Retriever.

Thinking It Over

1. Do you have a child who possesses the characteristics of a Lion? If not, do you know a child who does? What are his or her most obvious traits?

2. What are some challenging activities that appeal to the Lion child in your family? (If you have problems coming up with ideas, ask him for some.)

3. What trials have happened to your Lion child lately that caused personal pain or conflict with others? Discuss the trials with your child and how he can avoid this pain or conflict in the future.

4. Since these children are so goal oriented, what are some goals you can help them make to further their communication and interpersonal relationship skills?

5. What are some key areas you can praise your Lion child for? Try to discover at least one thing each day to encourage your Lion about.

6. In this chapter were you able to see the strengths *and* weaknesses of the Lion trait? Who in your family needs to either strengthen or tone down his Lion tendency? Do you need to do either?

CHAPTER FOUR

Connecting with the Otter

I can't believe it! I didn't sign him in." I stared with disbelief at Jason's name scratched off the 50-meter freestyle event.

Fourteen-year-old Jason had been invited to Hawaii for an International Invitational Swim Meet. And I, his own father (not to mention one of the swimming officials), hadn't signed him in before the start of the meet. Yikes!

Jason, our Golden Retriever, had enjoyed the three days with other kids from Australia, Japan, and New Zealand. The swim meet was a great place to trade U.S. T-shirts for boomerangs and other great foreign souvenirs, along with meeting kids from other countries.

And Dad, the fun-loving Otter, was too busy having fun at the beach with Jason to think about the mandatory check-in.

I went straight to the head referee and finally got Jason entered, but in one of the slower heats. And so without being able to warm up, Jason took his place on the starting blocks, dove in, and absolutely destroyed the slower competition.

He came in third overall, but probably could have won the event if he had been pushed by faster swimmers. (I'm not just saying that as a prejudiced parent. Jason did place first in the 100-meter freestyle—which I did manage to sign him in for.)

OTTERS JUST WANNA HAVE FUN

If you've seen otters in a zoo, you know that these fun-loving creatures personify perpetual motion. Into the water. Out of the water. Back into the water. Swimming in dizzying circles. Eating while floating on their backs and balancing their food on their stomachs. (Does that sound like one of your children? Your spouse? You?)

Now being an Otter is not something to be avoided. The apostle Peter was probably an Otter. He was outspoken and opinionated: "Hey, even if everybody else denies You, I won't!"

Certainly whacking off the ear of the high priest's servant—while surrounded by Temple troops—was just a bit impulsive. And walking on water was certainly something an Otter would have tried—if only once. But just like the Lion Paul, God could use the Otter Peter. And He did.

THE ENERGIZER

A popular television commercial features the Energizer® Rabbit—a battery-powered bunny who bursts into other commercials with its drum-pounding performance. That's a lot like our daughter, Jill. She's a nuclear-powered bundle of optimism and emotional energy—she "just keeps going, and going, and going . . ."

For instance, a few years ago we went skiing in Colorado. Jill took to snow like an otter to water. She could out-ski Suzette and me—even without any poles. Jill skied a bit with us, then got bored and darted down the slope by herself.

"Jill, don't get that far ahead of . . ." Suzette started to say, but by then Jill had disappeared into the blowing snow.

"Jim," Suzette panted. "I can't see her." By then the wind had turned the slope and sky into a white swirl. We felt our way along the trail—until it forked in two different directions.

"Which way did she go?" I asked, not expecting an answer. Both trails were blown over, covering any evidence of recent tracks.

"Jim, it's getting dark. What are we going to do?"

"OK, which trail would an Otter take?" I asked out loud.

"The most dangerous one," Suzette snapped, obviously losing patience with her two Otters.

"This one looks the most interesting, Suzette. It sort of weaves in and out of the woods. I'll take it, and you take the other one." I tried to thread my way through the trees as the sun quickly sank behind the mountain.

"Jill! Jill!" I hollered. There in the blue glow of snowy twilight was Jill—straddling a tree off to the side of the trail.

"Hey, look what I did, Dad!" She laughed. I heaved a sigh of relief.

She really began to laugh when I took off my skis to try to untangle her skis from the trees. As I stepped off the trail, my two-hundred-pound, six-foot body sank chest deep into the powdery snow. I managed to free her, only to watch her disappear down the trail and leave me struggling in six feet of snow. I can tell you, that wasn't fun at all.

Life is a lifelong situation comedy for Jill. She didn't realize the danger that she could have been in if she had been lost for hours or that I could have died from terminal frostbite if left out overnight stuck in a snowdrift. One of the challenges, then, of raising Otters is to instill in them healthy boundaries. Boundaries is a dirty word to the Otter, but it's something they've got to learn.

"I want you to know one thing, Jill," I said after I finally managed to crawl on my stomach over the soft snow to the trail, get my skis back on, and feel my way back to the lodge. "This is where your adventurous spirit got you into trouble. Big trouble. From now on, you *never* go down a trail without someone else!"

Even in her Otterish exuberance, Jill nodded solemnly in agreement. She had seen the almost tragic consequences of unrestricted Otterish behavior.

EASILY DISTRACTED

Our Otter Jill has a high energy level but a low level of organization—just like her father and grandmother. My mom is always so busy enjoying her family that it's practically a Thanksgiving and Christmas tradition for her to forget the rolls in the oven—until black smoke pours out from the oven door to remind her. She's also lost a few pot holders by setting them on the burner while the pilot light was on.

Think that's Otterish? How about this one: a close friend of mine missed his ten-year high school reunion because he forgot what year it was.

Otters are not so much forgetful and disorganized as they are so fun-oriented that details are low on their priorities. And it's their people-loving personality that makes an Otter such a beloved and noisy animal. People generally love to be around Otters. But that noise factor can sometimes get out of hand, especially with kids.

For instance, Jill can hold her own to the "snap-crackle-popping" of five cereal bowls with her constant chatter. One morning Travis (our Lionhearted son) roared out, "Jill, will you just shut up? I know the average female uses twenty-five thousand words a day, but please don't use 'em all before breakfast!"

I realized that I needed to step in at that point. "Both of you need to call a truce right now and try to understand one another," I said, trying to avert another breakfast battle. "Travis, I know that chitchat really rattles your cage, but just back off. I want you to apologize for your rude remark to Jill right now."

Travis realized his mistake and solemnly asked Jill's forgiveness. I continued with him, "Travis, you've just got to realize that females need to talk a lot—and that you've got to learn to deal with that now, while you're young. You're going to be surrounded by girls now and by women when you're older, so you'd better get used to it."

Then I turned to Jill and said, "I realize that you love to talk, but you've got only ten more words until breakfast is over." Silence reigned for a few moments.

In the uneasy silence of the cease-fire, I tried to help both Travis and Jill understand each other.

"Jill, you see yourself as personable and outgoing, but Travis may see it as talkative or manipulative." Her brother nodded in agreement.

I continued, "You think you're enthusiastic, but your brothers might think you're conceited. You view yourself as dramatic, but they may see you as spacey."

Jill stared at her cereal. Otters are thin-skinned, so I tried to encourage our little pup. "But that's OK, Jill," I said stroking her long blonde hair. "People aren't always going to understand you—or Jason, or Travis, or even me. I love you just the way God has designed you, and little by little you'll learn how to get the most out of how He made you."

THE ENTERTAINER

Otters draw part of their energy from being in the spotlight. They're natural entertainers.

Jay Norman is constantly telling his son James, "Now don't feel obligated to entertain our guests." But it does no good. Their eight-year-old son usually begins with a death-defying display of acrobatics off Mom's jogging trampoline, which he has hauled into the living room. Next it's magic tricks and then a puppet show. Even at three years old he wouldn't leave church on Sunday evenings until he could stand up in the pulpit and "preach."

As a result, Otters have lots of friends and are fun to be around. But they are often content to leave their relationships at a shallow level. They are frequently more interested in an audience—small or large—than a deep friendship. That's why it's so important to try to encourage Otters to assimilate other personality traits to make up for areas of weakness.

Fun-loving Otters have fears, too. They dread rejection and disapproval of their performances. And they often take criticism personally. That's why I tried so hard to encourage Jill after her Lion brother took a bite out of her at breakfast.

MOTIVATING THE OTTER

Otters need to feel involved with decisions—they like to influence others. Whenever possible, get them in on the discussion and planning stages. If they believe they have had a say in the plan, it will be easier for them to carry it out— whether it's a vacation or rules and consequences for behavior. We'll see how Otters can contribute to family goal setting in chapter 12.

Otters are usually strongly self-motivated, so one of the secrets in motivating them is simply not to "de-motivate" them. If you are an all-business style parent (which Lion kids love), you'll probably turn off an Otter. Take time to relate to them and affirm them before handing them a list of chores. And try to lighten up and have some fun; it'll communicate better with your young Otter—and who knows, *you* might even enjoy life a little more!

Keep in mind, too, that Otters' emotions tend to the extreme. When they're up, they are really up. But when they're down, they are really down. Because of this they're easily discouraged.

For instance, Jill was enjoying a new toy that splatters small bottles of paint on a piece of paper as it spins at a high speed. The art that results resembles multicolor suns with the rays spreading out from the center.

One day I was busy working on this book and wasn't in the mood to do an art critique on what looked like an explosion at a paint factory. But fortunately I caught myself before I crushed her spirit and ruined her motivation by saying something like, "Later, Jill! Can't you see I'm busy?" Thankfully, I used another response.

REDIRECTION

"Jill, that's really neat!" I affirmed. And then I tried a technique called redirecting. "You know, what you need to do is make one of these beautiful paintings for each member of the family. How 'bout making them in everyone's favorite colors? And then sign them just like expensive art."

"That's a great idea, Dad," Jill responded and then went back to her room. I was back to work in less than thirty seconds, and Jill was kept busy—and motivated—for another thirty minutes.

We've also tried to appeal to the Otter side of our children by making chores a game. (We talked a little about that in the previous chapter.)

For instance, chopping wood is not exactly in the same league of entertainment as Nintendo.® But our teenage boys love chopping wood. It's a challenge to put that piece of wood on the chopping block and then split it right down the middle with the splitting maul.

We began by making it as exciting as a television game show. I would announce, "I can split that piece in two swings." Then the kids would start calling their shots, the winner being the one who called the number of swings correctly. There were no cash prizes or trips to Hawaii—but a trip to the frozen yogurt store was a great motivation!

With a little bit of creativity, you can make any task something fun. For instance, while director of overnight trips at Kanakuk Kamp, I always dreaded blowing up my air mattress. One day as I was feeling light-headed huffing and puffing into the mattress, it dawned on me. *Why should I blow this thing up?*

"Kids," I announced to the group of eight, nine, and ten year olds. "Who wants to blow up my air mattress?" Before I knew it there were six in line waiting to blow it up. It was a strategy that I had learned from one of my camp directors, Spike White. "You don't *have* to do anything here— you *get* to do it!" he used to say.

We've even made washing dishes more exciting. Jill creates "suds creatures" in the soap froth floating on the water. Now you have to be careful with Otters because they can make a mess of things. But if you can make a chore fun, a challenge, or something the child can take pride in, then you've successfully motivated him or her.

Even discipline can be something fun. Let me explain. One spring break, we decided to vacation in the Canadian Rockies. We had flown into Seattle and were going to rent a minivan for the trip into the Rockies. After a long flight, the Brawner Lions, Otters, and Golden Retrievers were starting to sound like feeding time at the lion exhibit. I left Suzette with the kids and went to the rental counter for our van. However, because the NCAA basketball play-offs were in town, all the vans were taken.

When I arrived at the baggage pickup in an intermediate sized car, the growling and snarling erupted into animal Armageddon.

"That's it! I've had enough," I said. "Travis and Jill, you are going to hug each other until your mom and I get all this luggage stuffed into this car." Two pairs of eyes stared in disbelief—along with several strangers waiting at the curb.

"Hug!" I bellowed. "And don't let go till I say so!"

Travis and Jill slowly obeyed. Other passengers set their suitcases down to watch this family drama. After several minutes our Siamese twins began to shake and weave with laughter, and soon harmony was again restored. We still talk and laugh about it.

Otters, because they are so social, hate to feel left out. When they are misbehaving in a group, a time-out away from the action is a strong incentive not to repeat their wrong.

Fun rewards are also strong motivators. "If you'll help with such-and-such, then we'll be able to go to such-and-such an event."

I realize that for Beaver- or Lion-oriented parents, this sounds like too much fun. But remember, we need to respect our child's personality and work with it as a given—not something that can be dramatically changed.

DOING WHAT YOU OTTER

It's probably a dangerous thing to have an Otter as a camp director. But I've learned—along with Jill—that sometimes it's best to stifle your Otter and do what you ought to. Doing the right thing is tough medicine for Otters, but they eventually learn it's good for them. And I've learned to temper my Otterish urges, especially when it comes to my role as camp director and the safety of others.

To me it seemed like a great idea. Sure, it had rained all night, but that shouldn't put a damper on taking fifteen college-age camp counselors canoeing and kayaking, should it? OK, the water was running about a foot above the bridges along the river, but that would just make it more fun. I put these eager counselors—who had come to camp early for work week—in Swan Creek at 9:00 in the morning and then drove down to the midway point to take pictures of the colorful scene. Or so I thought.

Thirteen inches of rain that month had turned this normally peaceful stretch of water into a raging, storm-swollen Amazon. Treetops were sticking up from the surface of the water, and the bridges were creating dangerous undercurrents. As I arrived at the viewing point, I saw ten of the thirteen craft floating along—empty! They had capsized in the rough water. I saw several counselors clinging to tree branches with terror on their faces.

I had told the counselors to just keep going to the pickup point when I let them out at the launch site. What had started out as a three-hour adventure, ended up an eleven-hour nightmare.

After realizing the danger they were in due to my miscalculation, I kept saying to myself, *Brawner, this is crazy! You get excited about something, and then you don't weigh the consequences or really look at the details.* But thankfully we were able recover all the counselors and canoes and kayaks.

Through this experience and others I've learned my lesson regarding letting my Otter scale run wild. I'm much more Beaver-like in my outings now. (See chapter 6 for a description of the cautious Beaver trait.)

SAILING, SAILING OVER THE BOUNDING MAIN

Boating accidents are the furthest thing from any Otter's mind when he decides that it's a great day to be out on the water. But with maturity comes a tempering of the Otterish urge. Dave Jacoby learned that the hard way when he decided to take his family sailing on a day when a brisk wind was rising on the lake.

One man's "nice breeze" is another man's gale, but Dave didn't let that bother him. He convinced his tribe by overwhelming enthusiasm that they would love to go sailing that day. They were relatively inexperienced in judging wind and water conditions and trusted his judgment.

As they helped their dad put up the mast, unpack the sail, and other duties in launching their twelve-foot sailboat, Beth noted with some concern that her hair was practically standing out horizontally from her head. But she shrugged off her Beaverish thought and kept working, thinking that, like the old TV series, "Father Knows Best."

Ann, in her Otterish way (she's a lot like her father), was keenly anticipating the fun on the water. She thought her sister's wind-blown hair pretty.

Finally the boat was in the water, and while Dave stood waist deep in the lake, Penny parked the car. No matter that huge waves were smacking into the seawall nearby and spraying them like a fire hose; Dave helped his family into the teeny craft and cast off.

What followed was either tragic or comedic, depending on how you look at it. Due to an ill-timed shift in passengers' weight, within about three seconds the boat had flipped over and spilled the Jacobys into the surging swells.

They had their life preservers on, but when a sailboat capsizes there is a complicating factor; sailors call them "lines." They are the ropes used to trim the sail, support the sail, and other assorted tasks. And they were now everywhere. With things gone awry, Beth and Ann were getting tangled in the ropes, and Dave and Penny rushed to free them. But keep in mind that the rough seas were also involved, and you have a picture of true chaos and potential danger.

"Thank God, the boat had capsized near shore," says Dave. "That part of the lake was so shallow that Penny and I were able to actually stand on bottom and extricate the girls." Dave learned a scary lesson in not letting his enthusiasm get the best of his better judgment. He, too, is now a reformed boating enthusiast and calls forth all his Beaver traits whenever he gets around boats and water.

OTTERS AND A BAD CROWD

Since Otters are such able entertainers, they can ingratiate themselves with just about any crowd. But we must remember that sometimes they may attach themselves to the wrong group.

Such was the case with Tommy. Back in my years as a junior high school principal, I once caught Tommy lifting the acoustic ceiling tiles in the boys' restroom to get a peek at his female counterparts in the girls' restroom. Tommy was an adventuresome boy and had frequently been in trouble at the school. He wanted to be liked by everyone, and so when his pals dared him to do such a thing, he did not hesitate.

His response to me was typically Otter: "But, Mr. Brawner, I didn't see *anything!*" He conveniently ignored the other aspects of the infraction and focused on the thrill aspect. Deep down Tommy knew that this was a serious breach of conduct, and that I could expel him for it.

I chose, however, to recommend counseling for him. Through it he found that his Otter trait was in essence running wild and unhindered, and that this pattern of unrestraint was causing serious problems for him and those around him. Fortunately, he learned to rein in his Otter trait and consider the consequences when contemplating actions that seemed attractive.

PIKE'S PEAK REVISITED: THE OTHER TRAITS

Sometimes we forget that in reality all of us have all four traits within our personality, especially when one or two of them are evident in towering proportion. This became clear to me one day while I was in Colorado working at one of John Trent and Gary Smalley's seminars.

Otters at a Glance

Otters tend to like:

Anything fun

Opportunities to help and/or motivate others

A platform to inform or entertain others

Otters tend to fear:

Deadlines

Boring activities

Rejection

Otters are motivated by:

Recognition and approval

Fun

Challenges

Gary, who is an incurable Otter, woke up one morning and in his enthusiasm (Otters are often morning persons, to the dismay of the rest of us) enthusiastically suggested we jog to the top of one of the nearby (Rocky) mountains. Now keep in mind that in the spring, the mountains are like tundra—thawed out just enough to create muddy quicksand that keeps sucking at your shoes.

So there we were: John Trent, myself, and Terry Brown, their administrative assistant, huffing and puffing in the thin Colorado air, flipping mud all over our bodies with every stride. And all the time Gary's exclaiming, "Isn't this great!" He was not receiving hearty "amens" in return, but in his Otterish enthusiasm, he didn't notice.

I was saying under my breath, *This is really dumb. Why are we doing this, anyway? I've just ruined a brand-new pair of running shoes! My running clothes are so muddy—how will I ever get them in my suitcase to take them home?*

But I found the treasure in the situation, just as Norma Smalley would have liked. I realized in one of those moments that I was getting my blend of traits under control. I smiled to myself and thought, *Hey, I'm not a total Otter after all!*

"Man's best friend" is the slogan characterizing our next furry friend. Perhaps you've been blessed with a Golden Retriever spouse or child—a loyal friend and companion who brings a glowing warmth to your home. Or perhaps you're frustrated with a child who's overly sensitive and easily has his or her feelings hurt. In either case, in the next chapter you'll learn how to better communicate with and love the Golden Retriever in your family circle.

Thinking It Over

1. Can you identify anyone in your family who seems to be an Otter? Does he or she enjoy having fun and taking risks? Does this person have a problem keeping his room clean? Do you constantly have to remind him not to forget this or that? How do you react to him? Do you find yourself disliking this person's behavior (even if only slightly)? Has this chapter helped you to see his orientation in a more favorable (or at least more neutral) light?

2. What are some games your Otter child likes to play? Can you think of any games you could create that would help him or her accomplish chores or duties? What rewards or deterrents would motivate her to act responsibly? What are some helpful and creative reminders that would help your Otter remember tasks such as finishing homework, picking up clothes, and finding her hat or glasses?

3. When an Otter child is excited and out of control, it is important to remain calm. In such a situation, what could you do to bring the things back under control?

4. Because of their nature, Otter kids need at least one good praising comment from their parents each day. What have you praised your Otter for today?

5. In this chapter were you able to see the strengths *and* weaknesses of the Otter trait? Who in your family needs to either strengthen or tone down his Otter tendency? Do you need to do either?

CHAPTER FIVE

Connecting with the Golden Retriever

Just like a beloved family dog that loves children, Jason is an incredible babysitter—and in much demand in the neighborhood. This sixteen year old isn't the type who raids the refrigerator, plops on the couch in front of the television, and then yells to the kids, "Go find something to do so you won't bother me!"

Jason is down on the floor wrestling with them, playing games, and making sure each child is having a good time. He gets involved on their level and makes the time away from their parents a positive experience.

That's because Golden Retrievers are more interested in relationships than goals (Lions), a good time (Otters), or tasks (Beavers). Golden Retrievers thrive on interacting with other people. At first glance, Retrievers don't appear to be "people people." At a party, an Otter is scurrying around meeting everyone, while a Retriever may be off in the corner spending the evening with just one or two people.

But if you could listen in on the conversation, you'd find that the Otter limits himself to a social "script":

"Hi, I'm John Otter. And you are?"

"Hi, I'm Jane Other."

"Great party, isn't it?"

"Yeah."

"What school do you go to?"

"Wetlands Junior High. I'm in seventh grade."

"Really. I go there too. Well, great to get to know you. See ya around."

By the end of the party an Otter can recognize the faces of those he or she talked to but has totally forgotten names, grades, or anything else about the people he has met.

The Retriever, however, can tell you all that information about one or two people—as well as those people's favorite subject and teacher, whether their mom and dad are getting along, whom they have a crush on, their favorite music group, and many more details.

Otters tend to have lots of surface friendships, whereas Retrievers usually have only a few deep relationships. Golden Retrievers make terrific friends and spouses—you can count on them to be there for you when you need them.

THE SHIRT OFF HIS BACK

Self-sacrifice is a Retriever's middle name. That's why in a marriage you'll often find one of the spouses with a strong Retriever trait. Typically it's the woman, who plays out her orientation in loving, low-profile service to her husband and children. But sometimes it's the other way around.

Take Bill and Audrey, for example—a couple in Georgia who wanted to model the ideal marriage above all else. But the orientation they were given puzzled them before they understood their personality mix.

Audrey has a strong Lion trait, taking life's problems head-on and forging ahead with great tenacity, boldness, and courage. To her, the only way to approach life is to roar ahead, boldly addressing the challenges that present themselves.

By contrast, her husband, Bill, plays his role in a more laid-back manner. He is easygoing, dependable, and steady. In contrast to his wife, he rarely worries about a potential problem; he'll cross that bridge when he comes to it.

Yet for a considerable time before understanding our four furry friends, Audrey felt conflicting emotions as she considered their differences. On the one hand, she felt guilty for being too bold and in a way taking the lead in family matters, as Lions tend to do. She thought she was violating the biblical doctrine of headship and that exercising her Lionish inclination was dishonoring to the leadership of her husband. On the other hand, she felt that Bill's less-than-aggressive approach to solving problems was inferior, and this caused friction in their relationship, to say the least.

Audrey felt truly "between a rock and a hard place," since her natural approach to life was guilt-producing, and her husband's approach caused some disdain to well up inside her. The biblical injunction that "the wife must respect her husband" (Ephesians 5:33) haunted her. Yet with her current views she had no other logical emotion.

Audrey was, however, confusing cultural factors with biblical ones. That is, submitting to your husband's headship does not necessarily require a Lionhearted spouse to act like a doormat; it just means that the strongly motivated Lioness needs to rein in her passions on occasion, expressing mutual respect during discussions where she and her spouse disagree.

Similarly, her husband wasn't violating the biblical injunction to act as "head of the wife" (Ephesians 5:23) by approaching life in a predominantly Retriever-like way. Even though American culture tends to affirm bold action and degrade more passive action, one style is not necessarily better than the other; they're just different approaches. Audrey was confusing stylistic variation with substantive difference, and it caused her years of confusion and anxiety.

But when they both began to understand personality mix, they began to relax and accept the personality packages that God and life had created in each other, and the anxiety practically vanished.

Oh, you can be sure that today they both have to work on their weaknesses and control their strengths. Bill has to occasionally take a more bold and proactive approach to problems, and Audrey has to occasionally restrict her Lion-hearted ways. But they turned a significant corner in their relationship when they understood their styles weren't nec-essarily better or worse—just different.

JUNKING THE DOORMAT SYNDROME

That idea of the good Christian wife acting like a door-mat is more pervasive than you might think. Penny Jacoby, who has a strong Golden Retriever trait, found that out in relating to her Lionish husband Dave.

For many years Penny was mistakenly operating on that false assumption until, through the help of friends and an understanding of personality types, she saw the light. Her first opportunity to stand up to her sometimes overly Lionhearted hubby came when the vacuum cleaner belt broke, making a long black mark on the carpet. And to make mat-ters worse, company was coming over in half an hour.

Penny thought a quick solution was to move an area rug in the room over to cover the mark, but in her Retriever-ish way she asked Dave what he thought of the idea (Re-trievers like consensus in decision making).

Dave, in a rather hasty reply (Lions are given to hasty judgments), said he thought that the rug should stay where it was. It seemed to Dave that the guests probably wouldn't notice it anyway. (Lions are often too confident about things like that—the mark was indeed ugly, and the guests would surely notice it.) Assuming that he had just pronounced the perfect solution, Dave turned and walked into the other room.

Penny at first thought that she should submit to her husband in this matter, but the more she thought about it, the more she realized that it wasn't a matter of huge importance. *What would it really matter*, she reasoned, *if she moved the area rug a bit?*

Now you may think that this is a trivial story (especially if you're a Lionhearted male), but any hostess knows the anxiety that sets in when company is just about to arrive and something like this happens.

Penny cast off the doormat syndrome, bucked up her Lion trait, and went into the kitchen to tell Dave that she thought moving the rug was the best solution and that she had just done it. It was a difficult thing for her to do, but to her amazement Dave shrugged and said, "You're probably right." Lions may growl out the perfect solution and imply that their idea is the only one that intelligent people would consider, but they're also surprisingly quick to capitulate when they're given a bit of time to cool off.

Penny found that simple act to be amazingly significant and yet powerfully freeing. That's the way it often is when the strong, dominance-oriented Lion trait butts up against the cooperative, somewhat compliant Retriever trait. To a lot of Lions, Beavers, and Otters, her actions might seem trivial, but to most purebred Retrievers, what she did was a major step.

In parent-child relationships this is true as well—perhaps even more so when a Lion parent is relating to a Retriever child. Then the power balance is even more extreme, since the Lion is also the parent to boot. For example, one woman we know has a strong Retriever daughter, Valerie, who hardly ever gets out of hand. In contrast, her younger brother is a bundle of energy and a mischievous child who often needs correction.

The mother is often amazed that when she verbally corrects Valerie's little brother in front of her, Valerie straightens up her act, too. The little Retriever is so eager to please that even though it's clear that the reproof is not directed at her, she tries even harder to obey! And if her little brother receives a spanking, Valerie is often moved to tears. Why? Strong feelings of empathy. This behavior is typical of Golden Retrievers. As I often say, they're just a big heart with legs. They often side with the underdog.

Such extreme sensitivity can either be a blessing or a curse, depending on its level and the mix with other personality factors. Regardless of the mix, parents need to remember that nurturing our children is "job one," as the automobile commercial goes.

THE LOYAL, STEADY RETRIEVER

Not only do Retrievers want steady, secure relationships, they hunger for daily patterns and consistent, familiar surroundings as well. They don't adjust well to change—such as a move to another town, a divorce, a new school, or even the addition of a new sibling to the family. They tend to thrive on routine and predictability; they are truly creatures of habit.

Again, that can be either positive or negative. The positive side is dependability; the negative side is often a resistance to change—even positive change. They often grow up to be the church board member whose favorite line is, "We've never done it that way before. Why should we change now?"

Part of the reason they dislike change is their intense loyalty to people. A move out of state threatens those relationships that they have come to depend upon and from whom they draw emotional energy.

For instance, when Suzette and I moved from Harrison to Little Rock, Arkansas, we went from a rural community to a fast-paced metropolitan area. Suzette took a teaching job to supplement our income. This also meant that three-and-a-half-year-old Jason and one-and-a-half-year-old Travis had to attend a preschool.

For Jason, every morning was a traumatic experience when he was left at the school. In contrast, our Lion, Travis, couldn't wait to get to school for all the activities.

Jason felt that he had been deserted by his mother and by his own brother, who was off having a ball with other kids. The year was a time of anxiety and stress for Jason, who had been ripped away from his hometown, his mother, and Travis.

As a result, Suzette started a gymnastics school, which allowed her to schedule her work hours to spend more time with the boys and provide Jason with a more consistent and controlled environment. That was one of the best decisions we ever made.

Kids desperately need at least one full-time parent, and I believe we should move mountains to provide all the support we can, especially during those early years, regardless of our kids' personality mix.

Even today Suzette works part-time as the sales manager for a sportswear line that benefits a nonprofit portion of our camp ministry. She travels to New York City three times a year to meet with buyers of large department store chains, but most of the time is available to our three kids (not to mention me).

Difficulty with Sudden Change

Disrupted relationships are difficult for Golden Retrievers to handle, and unexpected change of any type is also tough. That's why it's important to preview any change well in advance and allow Retrievers to process that information. Then introduce the actual change at a later date, when appropriate.

A few years ago, I was being interviewed by another company, which would have meant relocation for our family. During the time Suzette and I were considering this option, we kept the details to ourselves, not wanting to unduly upset our children with such a difficult decision (especially if I ended up not taking the position).

This was especially true for Jason, our Golden Retriever, who was thirteen at the time. During the latter stages of our consideration process, I began to prepare Jason for the actual family discussion of this critical decision by asking leading questions: "Do you think my talents are being used to their fullest in the camp setting?" and, "Are you able to visualize me ever doing any other work than directing camp?"

Then when we actually shared the opportunity at a family meeting, we asked questions such as, "How do you think this decision would affect you?" and, "What opportunities would you see in this new situation?" and, "What are the pros and cons of this decision from your point of view?"

Having prepped Jason for this discussion with both advance warning (Retrievers like to mull things over for a while) and probing questions undoubtedly helped him with the transition. As it turned out, I ended up not accepting the offer, but we learned the value of preparing our kids and allowing them to have a part in the decision-making process.

CAUTION: RETRIEVERS MOVE SLOWLY

Because of this need for familiar patterns, Retrievers don't make quick decisions . . . or, for that matter, do anything quickly. For instance, Jason punches the "snooze" button on his alarm clock two or three times before getting up. Travis the Lion, however, is out of the bed, has it made, and is into the shower before the alarm's sound waves have reached Jason.

That's why we have different wake up times for each temperament. We give Jason lots of time, because the more you pressure a Retriever to hurry, the slower he becomes. Now both are ready at the same time, even though they do not start at the same time. Without taking this into consideration, frustration results for both parent and child.

Golden Retrievers, for all their lovableness, are easy to misunderstand, as Jill (the Otter) and Travis (the Lion) can testify. Whereas Jason thinks of himself as agreeable, Travis sometimes views him as being wimpy. Jason thinks of himself as dependable and reliable, whereas Jill may on occasion think he's boring. Many of our family meetings revolve around trying to understand each others' unique personality mix, as we shared in the last chapter. We'll discuss the importance of family meetings more fully in chapter 12.

MOTIVATING GOLDEN RETRIEVERS

Acceptance of and harmony with others are the strongest motivators for the Golden Retriever. But that inbred desire can make Retrievers and Otters easy targets for peer pressure or drugs, cults, or illicit sexual activities.

Fortunately Jason and his mother draw the line at making people happy when it comes to standards. They crave harmony, but not badly enough to compromise principles of right and wrong.

For instance, when Jason was thirteen he was invited to a fancy birthday party at a country club. We didn't realize, however, that a raunchy R-rated movie was going to be a part of the party.

But as soon as Jason realized what kind of film it was, this loyal, conforming, keep-everyone-happy Retriever got up and walked out of the room.

When the hostess asked why he was leaving, Jason softly answered, "Would it be OK if I went into that room and read magazines or something rather than watching the movie?"

The shocked hostess stammered, "Ah . . . sure . . . I . . . ah . . . I. . . . " As she began to regain her composure, another child came up to her and said, "Can I be excused, too?"

When Suzette later found out about the incident, she asked our son, "Jason, were you embarrassed to go up and ask her?"

"No, Mom," our Lionhearted Retriever answered. "She was embarrassed for letting such a lousy movie be shown at the party."

The apostle John was probably the Golden Retriever type who could also roar. We see John leaning against Jesus' chest at the Last Supper. We read it in the loving, relationship-centered book of 1 John. But we also see a Retriever who was called a "Son of Thunder" and stood up to the religious authorities (Mark 3:17).

The example of John points out once again the importance of not pigeonholing people. We are all blends of all four personality traits. And that's why it's so important to keep an open and honest relationship and encourage quality communication with your Golden Retriever children (Retriever parents need it too).

Golden Retrievers tend to be good listeners, but often parents have to draw them out by asking them questions and getting their opinions. Then we can hear and see what they're really feeling, rather than carrying on a conversation with ourselves because they're such good listeners.

Suzette, having a strong get-to-the-point Lion tendency, has had to learn to take time with Jason. Instead of a quick "How was your day?" she sits beside his bed. When he was younger, she would lie down beside him.

Now Suzette knows a lot of what's going on in Jason's life because she takes time to draw him out. He'll open up about how he's feeling, what he's discouraged about, his dating relationships, phone conversations—he pours his heart out.

Suzette is also careful not to close Jason off by expressing anger or shock. She allows herself to feel those emotions when appropriate, but she tries not to express them around tenderhearted Jason. The best strategy, she says, is to hold those feelings inside until you get to your room and "then just scream into your pillow!" After you've expressed the feelings and calmed down a bit, you can bring the subject up again and talk calmly about it with your Golden Retriever.

God's Compassionate Gift

As I write this, my son Jason is sixteen years old and towers over his mother at six foot, three inches tall. But not too long ago (as we parents so often muse) he was only five. We were living in Little Rock, and Suzette realized that the house was awfully quiet. Know the feeling? It feels good at first, yet then panic threatens to rear its ugly head when you begin to imagine where your kids could be or what mischief they have got into.

That was true with Suzette as she realized that she hadn't seen her son in about half an hour. She frantically searched all through the house but to no avail. Jason was gone.

She dashed to the back windows and searched the backyard feverishly. Then to the front of the house, only to get a glimpse of him near the street, sitting down at the curbside. Praying in desperation for him not to go into the street before she could reach him, she ran out front.

When she got close enough to assess the situation, she slowed down as she overheard her little boy.

Golden Retrievers at a Glance

Golden Retrievers tend to like:

A few deep friendships

Regular, predictable patterns
in daily life

Clearly defined rules and goals

Golden Retrievers tend to fear:

Unplanned changes

The unknown

Loss of stability

Golden Retrievers are motivated by:

Loyalty to people and programs

Acceptance by others

Jason was holding a carrot (which he had evidently pilfered from the refrigerator) and talking to a dead squirrel. The poor creature had been squashed by a car, and Jason was trying to revive it.

"Here ya go, little feller—here's some food so you can feel better," intoned Jason. "Eat the carrot, 'cuz Mommy says veg'tbls is good for you."

Suzette's quiet chuckling soon turned to welled-up tears of love for God's gracious gift to our family: sensitive and compassionate Jason, our Golden Retriever.

Next we turn from the gentle and cooperative Golden Retriever to the somewhat more demanding Beaver. Beavers have high standards—for themselves *and* others. If you have a child (or a mate) who's hard on herself or who may even tend toward perfectionism, you'll especially want to stay tuned for the next chapter.

Thinking It Over

1. Do you have a Retriever child (or know of one) who bonds tightly to one friend (sometimes even to the exclusion of others)? What is it about his personality that makes him so loyal? Do you view this as an asset or a liability? Why?

2. What characteristics make the Retriever child so easy to get along with? What are the pros and cons of this behavior pattern for that child?

3. Why do you think a Golden Retriever usually has problems starting and completing tasks? Can you think of some relational methods that would motivate him or her in this area?

4. When reproving or disciplining a Retriever, have you ever noticed his nonverbal communication (for example, body language and facial expression)? What do you think his or her personality orientation has to do with such signals? Have you experienced the crushing of a Retriever's spirit under harsh discipline? Can you think of softer, more effective, ways you could motivate him to change undesirable behavior?

5. In this chapter were you able to see the strengths *and* weaknesses of the Golden Retriever trait? Who in your family needs to either strengthen or tone down his Golden Retriever tendency? Do you need to do either?

CHAPTER SIX

Connecting with the Beaver

Y ou never really know someone until you travel with him. Such was the case with Julie. This intern at Kanakuk Kamp always worked efficiently and precisely. Reports were flawlessly typed. Her cabin was a model of cleanliness and organization.

But on the road, that wonderful efficiency and precision sometimes went totally out of control. In the off-season, our staff members go on the recruiting trail, signing up both campers and counselors for the next summer. Julie would often go with the team, and during our travels we often stayed overnight in a motel.

For the longest time we were always waiting for Julie to come out of the motel in the morning so we could get on our way. We couldn't understand what was always delaying her. So one morning Suzette crept up the stairs to peek in on our friend while the rest of us waited downstairs in the car. What to her wondering eyes should appear but our Beaver friend Julie making the motel's bed! Then, when she finished making the bed look perfect, she turned to folding her dirty clothes into her suitcase—dirty clothes!

Can you imagine if all the travelers in America made their beds upon leaving the motel the next day? All the maids would probably riot! I guess such perfectionistic behavior was a shock to us because there are no purebred Beavers even close to the Brawner family tree. We have just enough Beaver traits to keep us from self-destructing, but as far as maximum strength in that area, it's a puzzle to us.

But fun-loving Otters need hardworking and precise Beavers. As an Otter/Retriever, I realize I'm somewhat lacking in organizational skills. That's why I let Kay Holiday, who's codirector of the kid's camp and a purebred Beaver, care for my calendar. She creates a color-coded work of administrative art that precisely tells me where I'm to be and what I'm to be doing at practically every minute of the day.

When my associate Kris and I meet with Kay, she's organized and prepared, so we Otters and Retrievers know we're going to get a lot accomplished. She contributes greatly to the decision-making process, and we know she's got all the details figured out long before the scheduled meeting.

With her gift of organization, Kris and I get to spend more of our time having fun and relating to the staff and less time on administrative details.

Julie and Kay have been greatly influenced by that line from Mr. Rogers' children program "Take Your Time, and Do It Right." Doing something the right way is the driving force in a Beaver.

Beavers will recopy an entire writing assignment if they smudge one word. They'll "white out" mistakes in their private journals—documents that no one else will ever see. "It matters to *me*," they often say. And multiple choice tests are especially difficult because they want to be sure they've picked the "best" answer.

But unfortunately, Beavers can sometimes be oblivious to time. Their need for perfection causes them to often take much more time to accomplish a task than any other personality type. They also lose a lot of sleep, since getting an assignment right is more important than getting enough rest.

My guess is that Beavers also take much longer to date and get married than other personality types. I don't have scientific proof for this one, but there is a lot of anecdotal evidence that even in personal relationships Beavers "like to take their time and do it right." Ever have a friend that married for the first time late in life, say when middle-aged? It's not in every case, but very often that person is so meticulous that he or she couldn't find a "good enough" potential mate until, say, age forty-five! These folks are not anti-marriage; they were just taking their time to find "Mr. Right."

PERFECTION: EVERY BEAVER'S GOAL

Because their personality tends toward perfectionism, purebred Beavers may be the hardest to relate to. Whereas they perceive themselves as thorough and industrious, others may see them as critical and picky. Whereas they think of themselves as serious, others may see them as uptight and even moralistic.

For example, after a long hard winter most people rejoice when the weather begins to warm up and spring arrives. One Beaver I know, however, muttered on the first warm day in four months, "It's too hot today!"

And other personality types—particularly Otters—see the Beaver's need for orderliness as compulsive and obsessive. Otters can see hardly any reason at all to be as careful, thorough, and precise as Beavers usually are—but that's as much a statement on Otters as on Beavers.

If Beavers let perfectionistic tendencies run wild in their view on life, they can create for themselves an endless treadmill of misery. Why?

Well, depending on your personality mix, you may or may not understand this point. The other three personality types have never adopted perfection as a realistic and achievable goal in life, but high Beavers actually believe that they can attain perfection in practically all they do, and they endlessly chase that carrot on a stick. But life is not really like that, so we need to help purebred Beavers give up an overblown sense of perfectionism. High standards are great, but perfection is impossible.

CAUTION: THE BEAVER'S BYWORD

Beaver children can drive parents bananas with their extreme cautiousness. For example, the child may get a new bike for Christmas but won't practice riding that new two-wheeler until two summers later. Mom and Dad really stretched their budget to buy it, but it sits in the garage gathering dust until the hypercautious child feels it's OK to ride it.

Or take the strongly motivated Beaver child who won't jump in the deep end of the pool, whereas her younger (Otterish) sister is splashing around fearlessly. Now don't get me wrong; Beavers *will* ride and swim eventually—it just takes them longer to try new things. So in the meantime they build patience in siblings and parents—not a bad byproduct!

DOCTOR BEAVER

As we've said throughout this book, there are no right and wrong personalities—only those we understand and those we don't. Right from the start of his gospel we can tell that the apostle Luke had a lot of Beaver in him.

Many have undertaken to draw up an account of the things that have been fulfilled among us, just as they were handed down to us by those who from the first were eyewitnesses and servants of the word. Therefore, since *I myself have carefully investigated everything from the beginning*, it seemed good also to me to write an *orderly* account for you. (Luke 1:1-3, italics added)

Painstaking accuracy are great qualities for a writer and doctor such as Luke. Now I'm not saying that all M.D.s are purebred Beavers; Lions are great as emergency room physicians when decisions need to be made in a hurry. And Retrievers and Otters usually have a great bedside manner. But this Otter doesn't want anybody but a total Beaver to operate on him.

There are downsides to this persuasion, however. Because of their intense inbred desire for perfection, Beavers can become immobilized by fear of mistakes or possible criticism of their work. This craving for perfection maybe be self-imposed, or it may be unconsciously instilled by a Beaver parent. For instance, if a Beaver earns five As and one B on his report card, he'll tend to view the entire semester as a failure.

WHEN HIGH STANDARDS BECOME DESTRUCTIVE

Jan, the young woman I wrote about in chapter 1, is a prime example of Beaver traits pushed to the extreme. She blamed herself for the imperfect relationship of her parents. And her hopeless feelings led her to suicide.

Part of this pressure is caused because Beavers also tend to view their work as a part of themselves. They have poured themselves into creating what they consider is a perfect—or near-perfect project. So when a parent or teacher criticizes their drawing or writing assignment, Beavers internalize it as a criticism of who they are.

Because they fear imperfection so much, Beavers can have a difficult time accepting God's grace and forgiveness.

Special attention needs to be given to show Beavers just how much God loves them—regardless of their performance. Parents' unconditional love can help convince them about God's amazing grace.

> You see, at just the right time, when we were still powerless, Christ died for the ungodly. Very rarely will anyone die for a righteous man, though for a good man someone might possibly dare to die. But God demonstrates his own love for us in this: While we were still sinners, Christ died for us. (Romans 5:6-8)

Now that's amazing. Though our family has not been blessed with any strong Beavers, we still make it a point to stress to our children, "There's nothing you can do to make us love you more or love you less." Beavers and Retrievers need special help in this area; you really can't overemphasize unconditional love.

TEMPERING THE BEAVER TRAIT: OTHER TYPES

As we have seen, an off-the-chart Beaver trait can wreak havoc in a person's life, as he or she chases the impossible goal of perfectionism. But a moderate level of the trait can be helpful, both to the Beaver and the other personality types.

For example, Suzette's brother, Russ, is an Otter-Lion who has never considered himself to have many organizational skills. "I hate to file," he says with an Otterish grin. Yet he has in recent years learned to "sort of file" by making different piles of important papers. When he recently needed to find some important data to apply for a mortgage, he was able to go to the right pile and find the documentation he needed.

"I'll probably never have typed-in labels for my file folders, meticulously arranged in twelve filing cabinets in my basement like a Beaver." Russ grinned. "But I've learned to organize my chaos to the point that I need to."

Know the feeling? I know several other people who amaze their friends and relatives when they can dive into what seems to be an unorganized mess and find just what they were looking for. Their typical explanation? *"You* may not think I'm organized, but I knew just where to look."

Lions can see the usefulness in being organized and can use that as motivation to make themselves Beaver-like. If organization helps them reach their goals (remember, they're highly goal-driven), they'll do it.

Golden Retrievers also can see the value in being organized, usually in relational terms. All the personalities can build their Beaverish skills, but they tend to see the why through their own lenses. If you have a child who needs to be more organized, build his motivation through the lens that he uses.

MOTIVATING THE BEAVER

Make sure you've done your homework before approaching a Beaver. They need lots and lots of proof before they will accept something as valid. This can be an area of conflict if the parent is a let's-just-do-it Lion or a shoot-from-the-hip Otter and the child is a questioning, critical-thinking Beaver. Think back over some of your interaction with your own kids or spouse. Have you experienced this?

Beavers want reliable sources. If it's not in black and white or from a source they trust, Beavers tend to be nonbelievers. Although you need to spend time building your case, stick to the point and don't stray from the task at hand.

Also, give plenty of time for the Beaver child to complete a task or chore. (Remember, Beavers like to take their time and do it right.) When faced with deadline pressures, Beavers will often slow down even further.

Once they see the value of the task or rule that you have proposed, Beavers will usually stay with it until it is accomplished to their sense of perfection. You rarely have to worry about quality control with a Beaver.

A Case in Point

As with all four personality types, one needs to temper or balance the strengths of one persuasion with the strengths of another. For example, each summer at camp, we have lots of team-building activities for the kids. We combine skill-building games with a teamwork emphasis.

Just as in Marine boot camp, we have obstacle courses (fit for children, of course) called challenge courses. One of them involves swinging on a huge rope suspended from a tree from one wooden platform to another. Sound dangerous? Nah—the platforms are only inches off the ground. But the rule is that if you touch the ground on your way over, your entire cabin has to start the course over again from the beginning. So cabinmates catch each camper as they swing from one platform over to the next.

One boy whom I'll call Jeb had taken a nasty fall a few days previously and had hurt his back. He was recovering and was fit to do this activity; still, he was sore and taking things a bit gingerly.

When Jeb went to swing over to the next platform, his cabinmates missed him, and he swung back to the original platform. But he was low on momentum, so he didn't make it fully back to the deck. His friend Willy could see that Jeb might have a rough landing on the ground, and out of concern for his friend he leaped off the platform to catch him and prevent certain pain. Willy had a strong Golden Retriever trait (had you guessed?), and compassion for his friend was tops on his list.

At that point chaos broke loose. The high Beavers in the cabin jumped all over Willy's case, chiding him for breaking the rules, expecting that there would be no question as to whether they would all be penalized and have to start over. They seemed to ignore Jeb's sore back entirely.

The Retrievers countered that this was a special case and that Jeb's safety was more important than having to

Beavers at a Glance

Beavers tend to like:

> To take their time and do it right
>
> Clearly defined tasks
>
> Assignments that require precision

Beavers tend to fear:

> Deadlines
>
> Criticism of their work
>
> Risks (they don't want to chance failure)

Beavers are motivated by:

> Recognition and approval of their work
>
> The need to be "right"

start over. Can you picture the scene? Boys yelling and stomping in the dirt, pointing their fingers, each sure that his viewpoint was the only valid one. It was almost comical.

I soon saw that I needed to step in and help resolve this one. The whole incident reminded me of when the Pharisees tried to entrap Jesus by accusing Him of laboring on the Sabbath (Mark 2:23–3:5). The Savior's answer—"The Sabbath was made for man, not man for the Sabbath"—pointed out the fact that people are more important than a wooden obedience to rules, especially where mindless rule-following would hurt people.

I decided in that situation that I would affirm Willy's helping Jeb, given the circumstances of his injury and other factors. The entire conflict turned out to be a powerful learning opportunity for the kids. Precision in following rules is fine up to a point, but it's the mature Beaver who knows when to temper that strength with love for people.

It is important that we understand each animal in our family menagerie, and I hope you've had fun—as well as been challenged—as I've walked you through the four personality styles.

But insight into personality mix is not enough. In the pages that follow, you'll learn more about how to motivate your children to become all that God intends for them to be—no matter what animal they may resemble.

In my many years of working with young people in a variety of settings, I've found the following thirteen ways to be tip-top in terms of practicality for helping kids develop into the best people they can become. Our kids are going to be adults someday, and we want them to become all they can, developing into people we'd be proud of. After all, isn't that what we as parents are striving for?

Thinking It Over

1. Consider the following saying: "If you don't have time to do it right the first time, do you have enough time to do it again?" Next, consider its corollary: "Be the job large or small, do it right or not at all." Which family members would heartily subscribe to one of those sayings? In reading through this chapter, have you been able to identify the Beavers in your family?

2. Do you have a child or know anyone who is a diligent worker or is particularly known for his or her high quality work? How long does it take him to complete a project and get it just right? Does it ever get him into trouble when scheduling is important?

3. Why do you think the leaders of the Pharisees would be considered high Beavers? How do you see Christ interacting with them to temper their out-of-balance behavior?

4. If you have a Beaver child, what is his characteristic response to your asking him to hurry up and complete a task? Why do you think this occurs?

5. Why do you think a Beaver does not take criticism well? How could you make your criticism more palatable for your Beaver?

6. In this chapter were you able to see the strengths *and* weaknesses of the Beaver trait? Who in your family needs to either strengthen or tone down his Beaver tendency? Do you need to do either?

CHAPTER SEVEN

Motivating the Family Zoo

Travis's sixth-grade soccer team was trailing 2-3 with less than one minute to play when he stole the ball from an opponent and began working it toward the home net. As another opponent charged toward him, my son kicked the ball to his teammate, Jack, who in his position as a forward could drive the ball into the net and tie the game.

But Jack was out of position, and the ball went hurtling across the grass and out of bounds. I closed my eyes, imagining what would come next. As center midfielder, Travis served as on-field coach. And as a Lion, I knew that when he was under pressure, fur would fly. I had seen him in the past unmercifully chew out his teammates. One time he went so far as to go over to Jack, grab him by the jersey, and drag him back into position.

I cringed for Jack, who had just been chastised by the coach at halftime and now had blown a chance to tie the game. I waited for Travis to verbally finish him off.

"It's OK, Jack! Just block the ball when it comes back in!" Travis yelled.

I couldn't believe it. Lion-hearted Travis was actually focusing on Jack's feelings and not the game. Purebred Lions don't naturally back off. Once they smell blood, their instinct is to go for the kill.

"Be ready, Jack. I'm gonna feed the ball to you as soon as I get it," Travis encouraged. Sure enough, Travis stole the ball, then kicked it to Jack, who in turn drove it into the net to tie the game.

As soon as the game was over, I put my arm around Travis's shoulder and said, "Son, I'm really proud of how you've become more sensitive in the last few months. You had every opportunity to blow Jack away and take charge of the situation, but you backed off and really felt for him. I know that with your temperament that's hard."

"Thanks, Dad," Travis responded, "but just between you and me, I did tell him off in my heart."

I chuckled to myself, understanding a Lion's struggle. Travis had done well.

AFFIRMATIVE ACTION

Affirmation is the key to motivating any personality type. Try to catch your children doing right, and then really brag on them!

For instance, at Kanakuk-Kanakomo camps, I serve as director in charge of staff recruiting. One of the things that I stress to the staff of more than a thousand is that "there are no 'little losers'" at camp. If a kid comes in dead last in an event, but he gave it his best, he receives as many hugs and encouraging words from the staff as the one who came in first.

We'll discover as we discuss each personality type that Lions, Otters, Golden Retrievers, and Beavers all have strengths and weaknesses. If our focus is constantly on the negative, we will close off our relationship with our children. It much better to focus on the positive characteristics that they display throughout the day.

For instance, a school principal I know made a list of the school's "losers" each year. These were the kids who were doing poor academically and socially. He would secretly assign four teachers to each "loser," as well as letting the teacher know areas in which the student needed work. These teachers were to make it a point to make contact with that student each day.

"Hey, John, good to see you today. How's it going in biology?"

Initially the kids would just grunt or shrug. But the teachers would give them a hug and say, "You can do it. I believe in you."

After just a few weeks, a dramatic change occurred in these students who had felt negative about themselves and their schoolwork. Their grades began to go up, and they became more involved in school activities and with their peer group—all because someone was showing interest in and encouraging them.

Another element of affirmation is understanding how perceived personality weaknesses can be channeled into strengths. For instance, a person who is negatively labeled as "pushy" could be positively identified as "thorough."

AFFIRMATIVE CORRECTION

Affirming positive behavior does not mean we ignore negative behavior. We simply don't make a major issue of their wrong behavior as we do when our children do the right things.

Dr. Bruce Narramore makes an important distinction between punishment and discipline.[1] Punishment focuses on past misbehavior; discipline focuses on future right behavior. Punishment emphasizes how bad the child has been; discipline points out how good the child is. Discipline communicates that we don't want actions or words to spoil the great future God has for them. Remember, we want to motivate our children, not demoralize them.

That is why natural consequences work well for older children. Obviously, we're not suggesting that parents intentionally allow a small child to touch a hot burner. But rather than punishing a child for taking a bite out of the bathroom soap, allow the horrible taste and stomachache to do the job of disciplining for you. The motivation against further soap nibbling is built in.

In order to motivate future positive behavior, the consequence also needs to fit the crime. In this way the time out, loss of privileges, grounding, and so on, in themselves are teaching right behavior.

"If I hit my friend over the head with a dump truck, I won't be able to play with my friend for a while." (Not being able to watch TV for three days has no connection with the crime, so that would fail to teach proper behavior for the future.)

"If I pitch a baseball through the neighbor's window, I will have to pay for the repair." (Being banned from video games for a week fails to reinforce the rule not to use the neighbor's house as a backstop.)

"If I stay out past curfew, I won't be going out for a while." (Having to set and clear the table for a week is not a reminder to be in at the appointed hour.)

A wise horseman knows to give his animal freedom while still holding onto the reins. The horse knows it is free to make decisions, but if he starts to get into a dangerous area, the rider will gently pull in the reins until the animal is back on the safe path.

In the same way, good child rearing has loose reins. Use just enough pressure so that you can guide them, but not so much that you choke them. Just the right amount of control is the secret to guiding horses—and helping develop healthy Lions, Otters, Retrievers, and Beavers.

AFFIRMATIVE GOALS

A large part of motivation is allowing everyone in on goal setting. If each member believes he or she has had a say in a decision, he is more likely support the goal (more about this in chapter 12).

THIRTEEN WAYS TO MOTIVATE YOUR KIDS, NATURALLY

One of the overall themes in this book is that, given the right conditions, each family member will naturally be motivated to grow, learn, and mature. We all want to be successful and reflect God's image, which is built into us (Genesis 1:26). But due to our sinful nature and the world system in which we live, there are many roadblocks to growth in family life.

We have twisted the ideal world God wanted us to live in. But through the redeeming power of Christ's Holy Spirit, we can fight back and grow despite the odds (Ephesians 2:1-10).

In a sense, battling the junk in our lives that hinders our growth is what this book is all about. And there's no shortage of junk in our lives—personality strengths pushed out of balance to become weaknesses, life skills never learned, coping mechanisms that hurt others—all these and more get in the way of personal growth and the motivation we need to pursue life with enthusiasm.

Peppered throughout this book are many examples of what motivates (and "de-motivates") both kids and parents.

But before we get into a careful examination of what motivates the four personality types, here are a few more motivators that I've found help *any* personality type flourish.

1. *Make your kids' activities a top priority in your schedule.* One man I know grew up with parents who *never* attended a practice or performance put on by the high school marching band in which he played. He was an excellent clarinet player, but his parents never came to watch him. A deep wound of rejection formed in his heart that he is still dealing with today. He has a lovely family and is recovering from the hurts in his heart, but it's not easy.

If your child is participating in sports, or drama, or choir, or whatever, show her you care by making time in your schedule. Actions really do speak louder than words. And these days time is more precious than gold. So when you make time to attend and applaud, you're giving your child real gold in relational terms. Your presence is a strong nonverbal statement of your support and love (more about nonverbal communication in chapter 10).

And take the time to learn about their area of greatest interest. I remember forcing myself to learn about competitive swimming (which I never pursued as a youngster) just because our kids liked it. In fact, I earned certification as a swim official. My life has been enriched because I took time to pursue an area that appealed to my kids. Your life can be enriched, too.

One final word on this use-of-your-time issue. You can go overboard as a parent and never allow yourself time for *your* interests. And even though you might do it out of a noble motive, it's unhealthy in the long term for all concerned. So be sure to permit yourself some time too. This is especially true for full-time mothers, who can get burned out from so much contact with their kids. Husbands need to step in regularly and give their wives some time off, some time to themselves.

For single moms, recruit other dads or single men to roughhouse and do other activities with your boys. Similarly, invite other moms or single women over to spend time with your daughters.

2. *Write encouraging notes and hide them where your kids will find them later in the day.* This may seem corny, but it's a fabulous way to put a spark of encouragement into your child's day (or your spouse's, for that matter). A day at school can get awfully long, and when your child is reminded that she has people at home who love her, she can gain support and courage to keep going through the tough times.

Hiding encouraging notes can work in reverse, too. I remember the time that Jason was starting to get interested in girls, and his mom was having a rough time handling that. By "rough time" I mean the normal transition from sixteen years of being the only lady in Jason's life to having to suddenly share his attentions with several young ladies.

Well, Jason could sense that, and on Mother's Day he got a card for his mom that wasn't just your average card. He hid it in a place he knew Suzette would find it. Today Suzette treasures that card intensely. Below an illustration of a bear giving his momma bear a big hug, the card read, "Mom, You're the First Girl I Ever Loved!"

In the case of preschool children who can't read a card, you can adapt the procedure with a favorite toy, beloved treasure, or stuffed animal. For example, John and Cindy Trent use a little stuffed bear their family has named "Love Bear." Their preschool daughter Kari is likely to find this little friend in the bathroom drawer when she goes to brush her teeth. John says it's a joy to see her "light up like a Christmas tree" when she finds their hidden love gift.

Then Kari will return the favor. John chuckles. "I've found little 'Love Bear' in my shoe and in the pocket of my robe. And Cindy has even found it in the refrigerator!" Such family fun can go a long way toward strengthening vital family connections.

3. *Whenever correcting, use a "praise sandwich" to surround correcting words with affirmative words: praise-correct-praise.* In chapter 2 you learned that Otters are not detail-oriented, neither do they plan too far into the future. If you have an Otter, homework can be a frustrating and tiring experience. There can be great trauma as bedtime nears and his assignments are not yet completed.

Suzette and I have reaped the benefits of the "praise sandwich" concept as we've tried to help Jill grow in her weakest area—organization. Here's how it works.

We allow Jill to begin her homework assignments on her own, as she should. But she should begin early enough in the afternoon or evening to allow her some play time before bed (an important thing to Otters).

When she reaches an impasse on a particular assignment, she calls on her mom or me for assistance. Knowing that the problem is usually misunderstanding the instructions (most Otters are guilty of this, including yours truly), we first look at the work she's already done and praise her for that. Then we go over the instructions once again.

We help her with one or two problems or exercises and make sure that she has understood the procedure. Then we gently underline the original difficulty—of not paying close attention to the instructions. Sometimes Otters are too eager to get into the exercise (or to get it over with) and pass over the pertinent instructions.

Then we complete the time with praise for how she picked up the correct procedure, did some problems on her own, and is making great strides toward completing her homework in time for some play before bed.

4. *Listen to what your kids have to say as if it were the most important thing you could be doing at the moment.* Listening really is one of the most important things you can do. When

you consider what's more important—knocking off that day's to-do list or affirming your child—you'll start having a happier home. We'll talk more about this type of communication in chapter 11.

5. *Guide your kids in setting realistic goals, then help them implement a plan to accomplish them.* Remember, kids are people too. And they like to plan and carry out their plans just as Mom and Dad do. But sometimes life can be a bit scary for a little person, so they need you to hold their hand in terms of guidance and cheerleading. We'll discuss goal setting more in chapter 12.

6. *Help your kids see a positive—but realistic—future.*[2] We're talking about *hope* here. Sometimes life can seem overwhelming to a youngster, and we need to provide a hopeful look to the future, based on both God's provision and the child's strengths. If we can color their world with such thinking, motivation is bound to bloom.

I say "realistic" because unbounded optimism can lead to disillusionment if the view toward the future is unrealistic. In other words, if you allow the child to think he's going to land a Rhodes Scholarship when he's ready for college, you may be setting him up for disappointment. Better to challenge him to consider carefully what major he's going to pursue and how he can glorify God with that skill. Then let the particular college be chosen later, when it is time to make that decision.

This is parallel to the talk in the sports pages these days of the great disillusionment that young athletes are subjected to in our sports-crazy society. The wisdom here is to not let every kid who can shoot a basketball through the hoop plan his life around the surety that he'll land Magic Johnson's or Michael Jordan's job when he grows up. He had better plan on getting a good education and working a normal job, rather than having "To Star in the NBA" on his resume under "Employment Objective."

It's a matter of bringing our mature life experience, as parents who've experienced life, to bear on the child's future view, making sure that the child is thinking realistically. It's all a question of balancing unbridled optimism (which is characteristic of the Otter) and cautious realism (which is characteristic of the Beaver).

7. *Allow your kids to excel without the pressure of living up to your past successes—or your desired successes for them.* Don't fall into the trap of living out your life through your kids. They are unique individuals and don't deserve to become entangled in your unfulfilled hopes and expectations. The classic illustration of this, of course, is when the overbearing parent explodes on the sideline of the football game and rips the coach's head off "'cuz Johnny didn't get enough playing time."

Once we've gotten our focus off our own needs and wants and start working for the best interest of our child, considering his or her own unique makeup—both strengths and weaknesses—we'll be a long way down the road to family and parenting success.

True love is working for the best of another. And nowhere but in the family do we have more opportunity to experience this.

8. *Place the emphasis on the effort your kids put forth in any activity rather than their success or failure.* Realize that your children can't win at everything, every single time. In every competition there has to be a winner and a loser. Our task is to make our kids feel like winners no matter what the outcome. Encourage them to give any task all they've got and to feel good about that.

At camp I regularly have the counselors celebrate every kid's achievement, whether he's the first one across the finish line or the last. In fact, it becomes contagious, and the other kids hug and give "high fives" to the last one across the line, too. It's a matter of refocusing onto the individual's effort as the chief goal, rather than the placement of competitors.

9. *Allow your kids time and space to be kids.* Too much scheduled activity can cause burnout and even sickness. Likewise, too high an expectation level can cause resentment. Too often we start treating our kids as little adults, and that can cause serious problems later in life.

I remember one time the local TV station in Springfield, Missouri, wanted to do a special news report that they titled "Yuppies Pushing Their Kids to Be Superachievers." They came out to our home and shot their video. I sure hope they weren't disappointed.

First off, we're hardly yuppies. We're country folk at heart. But second, although our kids do tend to be high achievers, we don't put undue pressure on them to perform.

As Suzette said on the TV newscast (regarding Jill's working out with her swim team three afternoons per week), "If one of our kids wants to stop an activity, they're free to. We let them choose the level of commitment that they want to commit to." Again, it's a matter balancing your level of expectations with what's appropriate for their age level. The pursuit of excellence is a great thing, but not if your family ends up a charred ember in the burnout bonfire.

10. *Help your kids cultivate special skills in which they wish to excel.* In other words, play to their strengths. For example, if you have a naturally active and agile child, you might choose to encourage him in sports rather than chess. Conversely, if you have a studious, reading-oriented child, you might encourage her in academic pursuits over, say, mountain climbing.

But don't get me wrong—we need to encourage balance in our children's lives. Bookworm types need to get out-of-doors regularly, and wriggleworms need to study history. But keep in mind that you're doing your children a big favor if you can recognize their strengths and then provide settings to help them excel in those areas.

Variety, as the saying goes, is the spice of life. Applied here, that means we need, on occasion, to expose our kids to new areas of activity. Let them try out a new activity before you lock them in. For example, rent downhill skis and pay for a round of lessons to see if it "fits" before investing in an expensive ski equipment package.

11. *When you suspect your kids no longer feel challenged by an activity, provide a means to take them to a more advanced skill level instead of dropping the activity altogether.* Consider how you can enhance the present activity before "switching horses." This could include signing up for an advanced class, a tougher sports league, a summer camp tailored to that activity, or a more advanced piano teacher, and so on. That way you take advantage of the experience the child has in the field, and he or she doesn't have to start at square one in a new area of endeavor. Sometimes this strategy can lead to a real breakthrough and can catapult the child into a superior level of performance.

This is especially true in children with Lion characteristics. Our son Travis thrives on challenge. For instance, his interest in soccer began to wane as he acquired a higher skill level while competing in intramurals. Rather than drop the sport altogether, however, we discovered club soccer. This more advanced level of competition renewed the challenge that Travis needed to further sharpen his skills.

12. *If your kids feel they have failed in an activity, empathize with them about one of the failures you have experienced—and survived.* Kids can tend to think that their parents always have success in all the things they do. We seem like super heroes to them, and sometimes it helps if we share stories out of our childhood when we failed miserably. It helps them feel OK when they try something and don't get it perfect the first time.

One night at bedtime, Dave Jacoby told his daughters how he succumbed to peer pressure and got in trouble for shoplifting as a youngster. Ever since, they've frequently asked their dad to retell it.

"I think I was about ten years old, and my little pal dared me to go steal some candy with him at a convenience store," recalls Dave with a wry smile. "I knew it was wrong and teetered on the edge of decision, but in the end I wanted to impress my buddy, so I agreed to do it." Dave has a high Otter scale (see chapter 4), which predisposes him to follow such plans put forth by peers.

"When the shopkeeper caught us loitering about the candy section and then trying to slip out unnoticed, he nabbed us. Just to teach us a lesson we'd never forget, he called the sheriff, who took us home to our parents.

"I'll never forget the shame I felt when my parents opened the front door and there I stood with the sheriff at my side. That really taught me an important lesson about right and wrong." Dave uses that story primarily to teach his kids about the dangers of peer pressure, but he also uses it to model that we all have sin natures and that we must beware of letting them get out of control.

My point here is that you have a wealth of experiences in life to draw upon to teach and encourage your kids. And you should take advantage of those resources. Kids have memories like elephants when it comes to your childhood stories. So tell your kids what it was like for you to have been a kid once. That'll really help them when it gets tough for them being a kid.

13. *If all else fails, simply ask, "How can I help?"* We all want to have the perfect solution for every crisis, but sometimes it's just not possible. So I encourage parents to keep in their hip pocket a one-size-fits-all solution for those moments when a plan doesn't leap into your head: ask your

child, "How can I help?" Often they know exactly what they need better than we do.

In the next chapter we'll examine a real application of this material: just how do parents cope with a family made up of different-aged kids? For example, when you've got teenagers in the same menagerie as preschoolers, you've got to do some fancy gear shifting. We'll look at how to best adapt your parenting style to make the connection with various age groups.

Notes

1. Bruce Narramore, *Help! I'm a Parent* (Grand Rapids: Zondervan, 1972).
2. This is adapted from one of the central themes of *The Blessing*, by Gary Smalley and John Trent (Nashville: Thomas Nelson, 1986), pp. 81-96.

Thinking It Over

1. What are some unusual and surprising ways you can praise and encourage your children (for example, notes in a lunch box, flowers, or balloons)?
2. How much time per week do you spend at your kids' activities? Do you think this is adequate? Do they?
3. What do you do to reinforce and encourage your child after a disappointing defeat or a poor performance? What method would most fit his or her personality mix? Do you need to do more of this?
4. Are there any areas of control that you are holding onto intensely? How could you loosen the reins (without dropping them)? (If you draw a blank on this one, try asking friends for suggestions.)
5. In contrast to grasping the reins too tightly, are there any areas in your family in which there is a total lack of self-control? What can you do to get a grip on the situation? (Again, consult friends who seem to have this area balanced if you have difficulty strategizing on this subject.)

CHAPTER EIGHT

Appreciating Age-Level Differences

The Brawner Family Zoo doesn't visit malls. It prowls them. Like hungry carnivores, my children stalk these modern hunting grounds for some new quarry.

Today's hounded game was feeding on quarters in the darkness of the video arcade. Jason and Travis had come well-armed with pockets full of ammunition to track it down and defeat it.

"Daaaaaaaad!" Jill howled as her brothers hurried off down the walkway. "Why can't I go too?"

I held tightly to her hand as our eight year old struggled to get free and race after her brothers.

"You're too young, Jill," I tried to explain.

"I am not! I can reach where you put the money in, and I can reach the joystick," she argued.

"I know you're old enough to play the games, but you're not responsible enough to go to the arcade by yourself."

Jill stopped tugging on my weary arm and looked puzzled. "What's 'responsible'?"

I explained that being responsible included turning off the light in her room when she leaves or feeding Josie, our dog, without being asked.

"Oh."

That was the end of our discussion, but we were delighted when Jill began turning off her light and feeding the dog without being asked. Several months later, she was enjoying our small town mall with her brothers.

One of the many challenges of taming the family zoo is using the appropriate direction and discipline at different stages of the child's development. Obviously, I will relate to sixteen-year-old Jason in a different way than I'll deal with ten-year-old Jill.

Let's look at the various personality types as they are cross-referenced with three phases of age difference. For ease of reference, I'll divide our parenting years during our kids' childhood into three age phases: preschool (from birth to age five); school age (ages five to twelve); and teenagers (ages thirteen to eighteen). We'll look briefly at the various unique conditions of each age phase, then look at the four personalities under each phase.

UNDERSTANDING THE PRESCHOOLER

Preschoolers' attention spans are roughly one minute for each year of age. (Some parents may question that it's that long!) These are what some have called the "make it or break it" years. Research and experience tells us that the bulk of a child's values, outlook on life (what's trustworthy, what's frightening), and even his vocabulary is established in large measure by age six.

Their basic spiritual values are also well established. At this age, children are able to understand how to please God, that the Bible is God's Book, and that the church is His house. Preschoolers perceive God as a real and loving Person and can begin to pray intelligently.

The young child's thinking is concrete, so he learns best through his five senses. He is generally at the first stage in moral development: discipline and obedience orientation.[1] This stage is summed best by "If it feels good, do it. If not, don't."

Willfully throwing my full bowl of cereal on the floor is followed by pain across my backside. Cross off throwing full bowls of cereal on the floor as a feel-good activity. On the other hand, if I manage to get half a spoon of cereal in the near vicinity of my mouth, I get an ecstatic hug and praise from Mom and Dad. I'll do that again, the child thinks.

SHARE AND SHARE ALIKE

One of the important lessons that can be learned during this stage is sharing. Kris Cooper, boys' camp director, uses the buddy system with his own children. All members of the family are our buddies. When siblings want to play with the same toy at the same time, Kris says, "We're all buddies. So, it's OK to let our buddy play with 'our' toy for a while."

Kris prefers this method to saying, "OK, you play with it for five minutes, then let your brother play with it for five minutes." The buddy system emphasizes warmth and love, something the simple time-sharing system lacks. (I recommend that the time-share method be used only as a last resort.)

As soon as the child can understand words and ideas, be sure to explain the "whys" of your decisions. This will do two things. First, it will force you to think through exactly why you have decided a certain way. Second, it will provide your children with a good model of how parents make decisions.

No matter the age of the child, inform the baby-sitter or caregiver of some of the basic house rules and discipline procedures. This is particularly important if both parents work outside the home and the caregiver is with the child for long and regular periods of time. The child who is exposed to several styles of discipline can become confused and feel insecure when the rules are constantly changing.

LION PRESCHOOLERS

As you might expect, little Lions are just big Lions in miniature. They are the go-getters in a group of youngsters. They're first in line, first to answer a question or riddle, and even first to plop their mat down at preschool when it's nap time.

They tend to have lots of questions for Mom or Dad, which can sometimes get tiresome, as any parent knows. Lion preschoolers are the exact embodiment of Dr. Dobson's by-now-famous "strong-willed child." Sometimes parents (especially mothers) pine for a cooperative child, but we need to remember that God has created our kids, and His creation is always good (Genesis 1:31)—even when He has seen fit to gift us with a Lion.

Be careful not to interpret a young Lion's questions, which often challenge the authority structure and the status quo, as out-and-out rebellion. Lions are not necessarily challenging you as parent; they may just be stretching their wings. If they learn to temper their strength of will at the appropriate time, they can grow up to be strong leaders.

In the young years, though, you do need to be aware that sometimes they will challenge your authority as parent. And then you need to come down firmly as the person in charge. After all, no matter how cute that little boy or girl may be, he's still quite capable of willful defiance.

If you're a parent with a strong Golden Retriever trait and a very weak Lion trait, beware of one of your Lion kids' controlling you. It might sound ridiculous, but it can happen. The Retriever parent must be especially firm when it comes to enforcing rules with Lion kids. In parenting it's generally true that success is a matter of balancing love and limits. But with Lion kids it's even more so.

OTTER PRESCHOOLERS

Perhaps the most important lesson that preschool Otters need to learn is the importance of orderliness. Left to herself, an Otter child will feel just fine about always having a bedroom that, as the classic line from mothers goes, "looks like a cyclone hit it."

Marsha and Richard Beach were blessed with two daughters who cover the opposite ends of the spectrum in this regard. Whitney has a highly developed Beaver sense, whereas Stacey is almost pure Otter.

Now keep in mind that these two girls share a room, and a small one at that. There is plenty of opportunity for friction when Whitney keeps her part of the room neat as a pin, and then Mom asks them *both* to clean up their room. Sound familiar? When differing personality types have to live in close proximity to each other, sparks can fly. Yet it provides an opportunity to learn balanced living.

Marsha decided to let consequences teach Stacey the importance of cleaning up after herself. She set the rule that both girls had to clean their room, make their bed, and get dressed before breakfast each morning. Failure to comply with this standard resulted in losing TV privileges that day.

As you might guess, high Beaver Whitney had little trouble with such a rule, but high Otter Stacey did. But eventually she got the message, and one day Marsha nearly fell over when she walked into the girls' room and found Stacey dressed, hair brushed, making her bed. And, best of all, Marsha was walking on the floor. (She normally is walking on the clothes that Stacey has left the night before!)

When Marsha let out a gasp of pleasant surprise, Stacey said, "Mom, I've decided that I'm not going to have a messy room anymore. I want to watch cartoons in the afternoon." Marsha and Richard poured on the praise over the next few weeks to reinforce Stacey's decision.

We can learn a couple of things from the Beaches' experience. One, constant moaning and groaning from parents has little effect—especially when the behavior fits with the child's personality type. Instead of ruining your relationship with your child by constantly complaining, use consequences.

And, two, customize the consequences to the child's personality mix. For a high Otter like Stacey, who likes to have fun as a primary motivator, the loss of a visually fun activity such as watching cartoons was significant. For other high Otters, restriction of time with their peers can also motivate, since Otters are such social creatures.

Remember to reinforce the positive behavior once it comes. Everybody likes to feel successful, and you can't overdo praise.

RETRIEVER PRESCHOOLERS

One of the unique qualities of Golden Retrievers is their sensitivity to others. But in the little pup this can manifest itself in oversensitivity. In other words, we have to be careful in dealing with them, especially if we're a Lionish-type parent.

Golden Retrievers can read nonverbal signals from Mom and Dad like a book. I remember that when Jason was young, he referred to "that look" as all the motivation he would need from Dad to reform. In general, you don't need to discipline Golden Retrievers as much as other personality types, due to their oversensitivity.

But be careful about sending too many nonverbal signals, or you could crush your child's spirit.

BEAVER PRESCHOOLERS

As we have learned, Beavers are prone to the affliction of perfectionism. And it's in the preschool stage that perfectionism can either be encouraged or snuffed out.

Beaver youngsters will take enormous time and care to, say, color exactly within the lines of their coloring book. And if they stray outside the lines, watch out! They'll quickly tear it up or crunch it into the smallest ball imaginable! Be careful to communicate to a high Beaver child that his or her acceptance is *not* based on his or her performance. Do everything you can to teach your little Beaver that while high standards are great, rampant perfectionism is not the goal. If left unchecked, such behavior can lead to a lifetime of misery.

UNDERSTANDING SCHOOL-AGE CHILDREN

As children mature, they become more aware that right behavior is more than simply what feels good at that moment. They begin to develop a concept of the "rightness" and "wrongness" of an action, and social pressure to follow the rules begins to develop.

The child begins to play cooperatively, as opposed to playing by herself while with other children. Though they are still essentially self-centered, they are growing in friendliness and in their desire to please other children and adults. Here's where peer pressure begins to get a foothold. Make sure to keep communications open; put it at the top of your priority list during this important period (indeed throughout the parenting years).

This is a crucial stage in the child's spiritual life. Older children can sincerely worship, obey, and trust God, as well as know basic doctrines. From grades five to nine, children are the most likely to make a decision to follow or reject Christ.

At this stage children can learn through natural consequences, as we discussed in chapter 3. Remember, we need to allow our children to fail occasionally, rather than bailing them out at every opportunity. By learning a valuable lesson in the failure, children learn to "fail forward," making progress even through their mistakes.

SCHOOL-AGE LIONS

Lion cubs by this age have a few of their teeth in, and it generally shows. In other words, they have an emerging leadership style that must be managed.

To illustrate, our Lion Travis entered second grade under a first-year teacher whom I'll call Miss Duke. At the time, I was the principal at the middle school on the same property. Miss Duke was a fine teacher, but she had what I call the "first-year jitters." You're just a bit unsure of yourself, and you give directions to the class in a hesitant manner. Plus, the kids are not accustomed to you either, so there is often a bit of a time lag between giving directions and carrying them out.

Lions are so accustomed to being in charge and having others obey them that it often bugs them when others don't "hop to" right away—even when they're not the ones in charge! So it was with Travis, even at the tender age of seven. Whenever he sensed that the students weren't obeying with sufficient promptness, he would bark out, "Hurry up!" or, "Get in line!" or, "You kids—sit down!" He wanted them to have sufficient respect for the authority figure, Miss Duke.

But Travis's behavior was dangerous in one respect—if he did it in an angry tone of voice, his classmates would resent him and not be his friends. So he had to learn to direct them in a helpful, friendly way rather than an offensive, divisive way. And he had to let Miss Duke learn to buck up her Lion trait! Most first-year teachers wind up learning that lesson.

SCHOOL-AGE OTTERS

Otter children in the school years usually are having lots of fun doing what adults call networking. In other words, they are having a blast with so many new friends. They seek to have contact with the maximum number of little chums possible, and this can occasionally get out of hand.

Like the time Jill wanted to have a sleep-over party for her birthday. We asked her to come up with a guest list, and she did: twenty-three friends were on her list! When Suzette finished picking herself off the floor at the prospect of that many giggling girls in her house, we discussed some more realistic goals.

Still another area of need for these Otter children is effective communication. Recently Jill brought home an assignment from her fourth-grade teacher, Mrs. Frazier. The students were supposed to replace what the teacher called "tired" words such as "stuff," "things," "good," and "bad" with more specific words or phrases. At this age it is important to teach our children how to effectively express themselves. Otter children, without knowing or even realizing it, may ramble on and on. We have found that asking Jill to explain a statement or word—even if we know what she means—has taught her to be more cautious with her words.

SCHOOL-AGE RETRIEVERS

The beauty of Golden Retrievers at this stage of life is that they can "put feet" to their feelings of empathy and consideration for others. They can excel at doing deeds of kindness for others, and we need to applaud that and let it rub off on the other members of the family.

Jason showed us his capabilities in this area when his Lionhearted brother Travis injured himself in a biking accident. Due to Travis's complete and total lack of fear (common to both boys and Lions), he earned the early nickname of "an accident waiting to happen." Do you have a little cub like that?

We lived on the crest of a hill at that time. (Travis was seven, Jason was nine, and Travis loved to race down the hill on his bike and, just at the right moment at the crest of the hill, do an airborne Evil Knievel leap.) What happened one day still makes me shudder.

Our little daredevil pushed his bicycle to the maximum that day and leaped into the air with unusual speed. Unfortunately, he got off to a crooked start. While airborne, he crashed into the pillar that separated our two-car garage. Jason yelled for Mom to come to the rescue, and she rushed him to the hospital to get stitches in his chin.

Throughout the ordeal, sensitive Jason experienced tremendous empathy with his fallen comrade brother. While we were at the hospital, he decorated Travis's twisted bike with a sign saying "Welcome Home" and tied streamers and candy on it. That sight really encouraged Travis after a traumatic afternoon.

Today Jason continues such acts of kindness; it's a powerful example of love in action. Retrievers have a way of demonstrating to the other personality types their need for showing love and compassion to others.

SCHOOL-AGE BEAVERS

During these first years of school a young Beaver will often earn decent grades. In fact, they often are straight A students, given their predisposition for excellence. When there's a list to memorize, they nail it down 100 percent; when there's a procedure to learn, they're usually first to get it down. They can often be used by the teacher as examples of "how to do it right."

But, as good as this sounds, it can get out of hand if the child gets his or her "strokes" *exclusively* from performance, such as getting good grades. Parents need to be sure that they affirm them in settings other than one in which they perform well. Otherwise they will grow up with a performance-based mind-set, with an overdeveloped sensitivity for criticism. And that can lead to misery, since criticism and less-than-perfect performance is something that real life is full of.

Some friends told me of their first parent-teacher conference, during their Beaver son's first year in school. Their son's teacher started out on a positive note: "Your son does exceptional work," she said slowly.

The parents beamed. Little Johnny always cared for all the details in his chores at home, too. They were so proud of such a fine report.

But then the teacher shared the rest of the story. The parents' faces fell when the teacher exclaimed in frustration, "The only problem is, I never see much of his work. He's always working on it to make it better and hardly ever turns it in."

No one can be perfect, and our children (as well as we ourselves) will be setting ourselves up for disappointment if we navigate through life with a perfectionistic orientation.

UNDERSTANDING TEENS

CONTRACTING FOR NEW PRIVILEGES

A teen's brain is hungering for new information. Teens are able to deal with some abstract thinking and symbolism at this point. Their sense of humor is developing, as well as their capacity for daydreaming.

During this time, teens are also developing what Lawrence Kohlberg calls "the social contract" and the notion of "universal ethics."[2] Social contracts are codes or agreements of behavior. Thus teens respond well to what I call "contracting."

Contracting is an exercise in give-and-take as parent and child work out an agreement for such things as curfews or other privileges.

For instance, like most sixteen year olds, Jason wanted a car. We worked out a detailed contract that listed privileges and corresponding responsibilities.

"As you know, son, with privileges come responsibilities. And the more responsibility you show, the more privileges you will be allowed," I began. Jason nodded his head, and I continued.

"The first responsibility you need to show before we get you a car is changing the oil. I'll show you how it's done, but then I want you to be regularly checking the oil in the family car. If it gets low, it's your responsibility to add oil.

"This first three months, we also want you to keep a record of the car's expenses such as gas, oil, license, insurance, repairs, and so on." I wanted Jason to realize the cost of owning a car.

We also established some consequences if Jason didn't fulfill his responsibility. For instance, Jason was financially responsible for any speeding tickets and any corresponding increase in insurance if any were issued. (So far, no tickets!)

CONTRACTING FOR CHANGE

Another way that contracting can work is in helping a teen break a bad habit. Most habits take at least three weeks to take root—and often even longer to break—so don't overreact when you see inappropriate behavior. It may simply be a bad habit rather than your child being irreversibly evil. And as a bad habit is learned, it can be unlearned over time.

So, contract for him or her to totally eliminate the habit in twenty-one days, the minimum time to learn or unlearn a habit.

Say, for instance, your teen is using crude language. A contract could allow three slip-ups the first week, two the second, and only one the third week. Establish consequences for each crude word over the weekly limit. As we emphasized elsewhere, make sure the punishment fits the crime. (For example, if it's a word he or she picked up on TV, cut out TV for a period; if it's a friend who uses crude language, limit the time they spend together, and so on.)

We've found this tapering off method much more effective than trying to force a child to give up a habit cold turkey.

We don't usually write out a contract, but we do want to make sure that it's clearly understood, so we ask our children to restate what we've just agreed to.

For instance, Jason and some friends wanted to ride their bikes to the hospital to visit Travis when he was laid up with pneumonia. I had seen how his friends rode bikes: no helmets, no hands, and often no direct route (somehow these boys took shortcuts that always wound up at the mall.)

I gave Jason specific instructions, and then asked him to repeat them back. Teens have so many changes going on in their lives that it's sometimes not guaranteed that they hear everything you say. So I often use this technique, especially where safety is concerned.

Jason sighed, then began.

"Right, Dad. Wear my helmet. Keep both hands on the handlebars. Don't take a detour to the mall. Be home by six o'clock."

Practicing communication and being consistent with regulations is important with a rapidly maturing young person. In this way, both parties knew exactly the terms of the contract.

LION TEENS

Lion children can thrive in the teen years, since they enjoy a lot of activity and challenges. The numerous offerings of schools in terms of extracurricular activities—clubs, sports, and so on—make a hearty challenge for Lion teens. They are becoming adults little by little, and, because they don't have to work full-time (if at all) beyond their schoolwork, these years can be a paradise to the well-directed Lion child.

But therein lies the rub. If parents don't guide young Lions and Lionesses into some healthy activities, they may end up in unhealthy ones. They are typically fireballs of energy during this stage of life, and you will probably be challenged to keep up with them. Don't be afraid to set ambitious goals for them either. Remember it's difficult to overchallenge a true Lion. Try to funnel their energies into areas where they can do well, and you will minimize the mischief that an idle Lion is prone to.

OTTER TEENS

Otter teenagers are often known as the "class clowns," due to their frequent comical remarks made at an opportune moment. Or should I say "inopportune"? Often an Otter, in his desire to be liked by his classmates, opens his mouth only to put his foot in it. He might think his quick remark was funny, but sometimes it can cross the bounds of kindness and hurt others' feelings.

Otters need guidance from us to learn when and when not to cut up. Help them see that there is an appropriate time to be serious and an appropriate time to be lighthearted, just as the Scriptures tell us: "There is a time for everything, and a season for every activity under heaven . . . a time to weep and a time to laugh, a time to mourn and a time to dance" (Ecclesiastes 3:1, 4).

Consequences can teach them a lesson as well. When I was a high school senior I learned the hard way that there is a time for everything. My Otter impulse was out of control as I drew back on a rather large rubber band that was aimed at the principal's backside. With highly skilled accuracy, my elastic missile found its mark.

What I in my Otterish immaturity thought was cute turned out to be a long and painful walk to his office. I was terrified—not so much at the threat of the shameful three-day suspension from school but from what I might get from my dad when I got home. Needless to say, I learned my lesson. Otters sometimes need to learn the hard way.

RETRIEVER TEENS

If by chance you have a Golden Retriever firstborn in your tribe, followed by the other temperaments, you probably got spoiled with that child and have wondered ever since what happened to the rest of them. Retrievers are good listeners and good friends. You may have to "jump start" them on a project (that is, show them how to do it and even encourage them a bit), but once they begin they do just fine.

It's important that you have a close relationship with your Retriever teen. This has a dual purpose. First, Retrievers need an outlet to vent their feelings (they feel deeply) when others let them down (they rarely let others down). Second, it will allow you to have input when they face peer pressure, a seduction to which they are particularly prone.

One mother said in exasperation, "My son Karl never talks to me! If I don't ask the right questions, I'll never hear what he's thinking." She was right in that Golden Retrievers aren't as talkative as, say, Otters (this mother was high Otter/high Lion). And in the face of interacting with a Lion, Retrievers tend to lay low. Parents need to resist the temptation to discourage this natural quietness and simply value the child's temperament, while actively seeking communion with their kids.

BEAVER TEENS

The teen Beaver has little patience with others who don't measure up to his high standards. Beavers can even turn on themselves. The teenage Beaver can, as the saying goes, be his own worst enemy, and parents need to challenge that. We need to point out a more realistic attitude than holding oneself to a standard of perfection.

Sometimes teens of this persuasion can develop a poor-me attitude that borders on depression. At that point we need to recognize it for what it is and counter it with some reality as it applies to perfectionism.

Most important, teen Beavers need lots of TLC (tender loving care). Lots of unconditional love can help tremendously.

What's scary at this stage of life is that, if left unchecked, out-of-control perfectionistic attitudes can harden into a lifelong way of looking at life. Remember, this child is almost an adult. So if your teen is expressing out-of-balance Beaver traits, get busy on tempering them.

WE'RE ALL UNIQUE INDIVIDUALS

As I've pointed out, don't feel guilty if you treat each child differently in privileges or punishments. After all, we're dealing with different individuals. Just make it your goal to be consistent with your discipline and regulations. And as always, balance love with limits.

For many people, the most mystifying aspect of interpersonal relationships comes in truly understanding the opposite sex. Whether it's parent-to-parent or parent-to-child, getting a grasp on gender differences can be of tremendous help in improving our familial relationships. We'll look at this aspect in the pages that follow.

Notes

1. Lawrence Kohlberg, "Development of Moral Character and Moral Ideology," in M. L. Hoffman and W. Hoffman, *Review of Child Development: Volume 1* (New York: Russell Sage Foundation, 1964), pp. 383-431.
2. Ibid.

Thinking It Over

1. At what age did you begin to grant increasing privileges to your children? Did any one child seem to be more responsible than another? Why? Can you see personality mix coming into play in this area?
2. If you have more than one child, how do you differentiate privileges from one child to the next? Is this fair for all concerned?
3. Have you ever caught yourself praising your children solely for their performances, to the neglect of expressing unconditional love? Have you ever praised them for just being your children?
4. What methods of discipline do you find most effective at each age level? Do you think you should make some adjustments to your disciplinary style after reading this chapter? Why?
5. Ask your spouse or friend to rate your relationship with each child on a scale of one to ten (ten being best). When you tuck your child into bed (for older children you may choose another setting), ask him where he would rank your relationship, using the same scale.

CHAPTER NINE

Male/Female Differences: It's in the Genes

C hildren not only come in combinations of four general personality types (which all act differently at various stages), but they also come in one of two genders.

It took coaching junior high track for me to realize just how opposite the opposite sexes are. For instance, I found that both sexes like to see the other gender in tank tops and shorts. But that's where the similarities end. Guys are there to show off for the girls and conquer. Girls are there to show off for the guys and relate to other girls.

You'll notice this most visibly during a high school football game. Upon a touchdown or other significant event, the guys will give each other "high five" and "low five" slaps, but generally remain pretty cool. Oh, they can show emotion too, but they generally save it for when they win the conference game or some other paramount event. They don't want to look foolish by celebrating every little score or tackle too much.

In contrast, the girls in the stands, those in the marching band, and especially the cheerleaders on the sidelines hug and scream at every turn of events. They chatter away about the assured victory. Only when the game's over and they are forced to go home do they stop their characteristic way of relating to their chums.

Thus we see a world of difference in the way the sexes relate. I mean, when was the last time you saw Lee Iacocca stand up at the end of labor negotiations and hug the other guy to celebrate finalizing the contract?

Some of these differences are culturally learned, but many are innate. Of course I could write an entire book on figuring out which is which (and still not find the whole truth), but for now let's just briefly cover some of the basic differences. Let's look at factors that will help us be better parents in understanding and relating to our coed zoos.

MALE AND FEMALE: THE IMAGE OF GOD

As we pointed out earlier, no one personality type is more godly than another. God is the perfect blend of all types.

In the same way, no gender is more godly than another. That may seem self-evident, but stop and think about how different segments of our society treat the opposite sex, and you'll see my point. Many feminists seem bent on destroying many of the traditional female traits. On the other hand, males seem bent on putting down females by implying that the male half of the population is more worthy than the other.

What does the Bible mean when it says that God "created man in His own image . . . male and female he created them" (Genesis 1:27)? One author writes that "God's character and personality are so wonderfully complex that He had to make two very different sexes to contain it all."[1]

In the Old Testament, God is referred to in both male and female terms. He is spoken of as "Father" but has also the interesting title "El Shaddai," which, according to many scholars, literally means "the breast, the one who gives nourishment."

And in Christ—who was fully God—we see a rough and tough person who clears out the Temple with tables flying and moneychangers running for cover, yet washes His disciples' feet. He calls the Pharisees "sons of vipers," yet weeps at the tomb of His friend Lazarus.

Although God's image is reflected by both males and females, most humans are born one or the other (unless you're the type featured in grocery store tabloids, akin to "Hamster Boy Born to Valley Girl"). Seriously, though, we must understand our little boys and girls to better relate to them.

ANY PARENT KNOWS

As any parent of both gender children knows, girls are talkers, squealers, and screamers, and boys like to run, jump, and throw balls through windows. My brother Jerry, father of three girls and no boys, says, "Having grown up with two brothers and only one sister, it was a real shock to find my three daughters screaming at the drop of a hat. It drove me crazy for a while, but now I'm accustomed to it."

Also, girls tend to emphasize relationships, whereas boys emphasize action and power in their play. One girl who baby-sits a lot said, "Boys and girls may both play with cars, but the boys are content to make 'vroom' noises, while the girls pretend that they are each driving a car, discussing where they'll go and who they'll visit." How true.

And one father who has both boys and girls marvels, "You know, I never had to teach my two sons how to make all those good boy noises—Bang! Vroom! Aaugh!—they just started making them one day."

When Suzette and I took our family to Colorado for a skiing vacation, we noticed the male/female difference right away. Contrary to what you would predict on a straight personality type basis, the boys (including me) acted a certain way, and the girls (including Suzette) acted another.

The boys couldn't wait to get to the top of the mountain and zoom down, hitting the highest jumps and going as fast as they could. Lionish Travis nearly killed himself when he went whizzing off a small jump and took off crooked. Thank the Lord that tree wasn't one foot farther to the right!

And Jason, the normally laid-back Golden Retriever, lacked no gusto that his Otterish dad displayed. In fact, that first day the entire tribe split up according to gender lines (the following day we stayed together as a family and did more tame things, such as cross country skiing and soaking in the hot tub).

In contrast, on that first day Otterish Jill hung back and skied rather slowly down the mountain, enjoying the scenery (and not auditioning for "The Agony of Defeat" segment of ABC's "Wild World of Sports" like her brothers). She didn't get bored, but she didn't push herself to the brink such as the boys did, either.

And Suzette played the "mother hen" role by taking it easy and warning me that it would be on *my* head if the boys broke their legs. She's a fairly courageous Lion, but she took it easy on the mountain that week.

LEARNED DIFFERENCES VS. BIOLOGICAL DIFFERENCES

Back when June and Ward Cleaver were raising the Beaver, society provided clear sex role distinctions: Dad brought home the bacon, and Mom fried it. Women wore dresses; men "wore the pants in the family." Real men were strong and rugged, whereas women were the soft, "weaker sex."

Boys were made of snakes, and snails, and puppy-dog tails, whereas girls were a blend of sugar, spice, and everything nice.

But all these artificial distinctions began to crumble when "Rosie the Riveter" went to work in factories to support the men who had left to fight in World War II. After the peace treaty was signed, many women continued in the work force.

At this same time, the modern women's movement began pushing for equality—not only in the workplace but in our culture as a whole. The more radical women of the movement declared that the sexes were "identical from the neck up" and anyone who disagreed was a male chauvinist pig who wanted to keep women in submission by continuing the culture's "sexual stereotypes."

If parents have both a boy and girl, they soon realize that there are bigger differences than just what color blanket they came home in. But what is biological, and what is a culturally learned difference?

Biologists and other scientists are discovering that there is an inborn difference between males and females—from the neck up as well as down. And, although comprehensive research has not been completed in the entire field, some preliminary results are worthy of note.

PHYSICAL DIFFERENCES

There are significant distinctions between males and females in addition to the material made clear by the charts in sex education classes. The following differences are observed in more than three-fourths of the adult men and women examined.[2]

An adult man pumps about 88 percent more blood through his veins than the average woman. In addition, drop for drop females have about 20 percent less red blood cells than do males. This means that men have a greater capacity for oxygen, and thus energy and endurance.

Men's bodies tend to be 40 percent muscle and 15 percent fat; women tend to be 20 percent muscle and 20 percent fat. Add to this the fact that men's bones tend to be heavier and larger than women's. Most men can out-lift, out-throw, and out-run most women.

But despite the apparent physical edge, a woman will outlive the average man by eight years. Women also age more slowly—even without Oil of Olay! Men age approximately 10 percent every ten years after forty years of age. Women age five times slower at a consistent 2 percent each year after child-bearing years. The brains of men deteriorate more rapidly than those of women.

Although chromosomes determine the sex of a baby at the split second of conception, at twelve weeks of gestation a male and female fetus look identical. At that point a male baby will begin producing androgen, which causes an amazing metamorphosis to a distinctive male body.

The higher level of androgen also tends to make boys more active. A study at Johns Hopkins revealed, however, that girls who were labeled "tomboys" had higher levels of androgen than other girls. Further proof came from UCLA where researchers discovered that women who took male hormones to prevent miscarriage gave birth to girls who thought and fought like boys.

At the sixteenth week of a male's fetal development, an even more amazing transformation takes place. At this time, many of the nerve connections between the two hemispheres (sides) of the brain begin to dissolve, due to a surge of androgen. Because of this, about 80 percent of males can use only one side of their brains at one time. Most females, however, can retrieve and store information on both sides simultaneously.

Research on stroke victims has revealed that men and women's brains are physically different too. Because men can't process data in both sides of their brains, a stroke tends to be more debilitating to a man than to a woman. Put in computer talk, in a stroke a disk sector of his brain has been damaged, and he has no backup. The data is forever erased.

MENTAL DIFFERENCES: IT'S IN THE HORMONES

As I pointed out above, there's quite a struggle going on in our society regarding sex roles. With some exceptions it is typically conservatives doing battle with more liberal scientists (both social scientists and hard science experts). But in recent years secular researchers—people with no axe to grind from a Christian viewpoint (often termed "religious bias") have been finding solid evidence about male/female differences. And, although the body of research is still developing, there *are* some things we do know.

For example, child psychologists at the Gesell Institute for Child Development in New Haven, Connecticut, studied at length the behavior of identical boy and girl twins.[3] They videotaped their play and tried to filter out all the cultural factors that could possibly influence behavior. Although they could not totally rule out learned behavior, they found that boys would typically resolve their conflicts with playmates by pushing, shoving, or yelling, whereas girls would want to talk it out.

Among other possible explanations, they believe this reflects differing physical maturation patterns between boys and girls. Such patterns put girls ahead of boys in terms of language skills; boys are more motor-skills-oriented at that stage. We'll see below that even when boys grow up to be men, and girls women, that this difference is still evident, though to a lesser degree. And that fact is evident to any observer, regardless of the observer's "religious bias."

A study described in *Scientific American* told of research done to track the effect that varying estrogen (the predominant female hormone) levels have on female performance abilities.[4] They were investigating whether the different hormonal mix that males and females undeniably carry could be the basis for gender differences.

The researchers found that when the women's estrogen level was at its highest (such as during ovulation during the monthly cycle), they performed significantly higher on verbal tests than during the rest of the month. Additionally, they performed most poorly on the spatial tests (tests where men usually excel) when the estrogen levels were high.

The significance of their findings? Put simply, when the maximum female factors are present (i.e., high estrogen levels), females perform better on the classically female-dominant tasks (verbal and fine motor skills). Conversely, when estrogen levels are lower, females' test scores on traditionally male-dominated skills (i.e., spatial tasks) are higher, more in the range of male test scores. So under maximum female conditions, females test out as more strongly female, and under minimum female conditions they test out as more strongly male.

The researchers noted above have done further work that examines body mass among men and women, especially looking at differences between right-side and left-side formation and structure. Have you ever noticed that your right foot is bigger than your left, or vice versa? Well, they have found that most people have asymmetrical body mass—that is, the right side is larger than the left (or vice versa). And, terming their findings "amazing," they found that men tend to have larger and more developed right sides, and women left sides.

The scientists hypothesize, with some degree of certainty, that this gender difference may be linked with brain hemisphere dominance—that is, that men have larger right-side bodies because of their left hemisphere dominance (remember that the brain hemispheres control the opposite side of the body). And women, being right-hemisphere dominant, would have a corresponding left-side body development. Of course, the differences in mass are very small, but in the early stages of the research, the differences are statistically significant nonetheless.

Thus it seems there definitely is something inherently different about girls and boys. (I knew it all along! My motto Viva la Difference is vindicated once more!) These results and more indicate that there is solid evidence available from a hard science viewpoint. They support the scriptural priniciple "Male and female he created them" (Genesis 1:27). Research will probably continue for many more years on this, but there have been solid, statistically valid studies done on certain aspects of the male/ female puzzle, and it's certainly legitimate to examine them.

MENTAL DIFFERENCES: RIGHT- AND LEFT-BRAIN DOMINANCE

Some researchers believe that each side of the brain has somewhat specialized functions. For instance, the left side is more verbal/linear-oriented, whereas the right side is more visual/spatial-oriented. In general, males tend to be left-brain dominant, and females tend to be right-brain dominant. But since females have a greater number of nerve connections between the hemispheres, they can more easily access both of these sides simultaneously. So in a sense females tend to be switch hitters, using either side when the occasion requires it.

This ability to more easily use both sides of the brain than can males may help explain women's uncanny ability to come up with a correct answer or assessment to a difficult, complex question and yet not be able to give males a

logical, sequential explanation. Some call it women's intu-
ition.

Suzette has plenty of this: "I just know it's right," she'll
say when she instantly solves a problem I've been struggling with for hours.

"But how did you come up with that answer?" I'll que-
ry, puzzled and a little jealous.

"I don't know. It just came to me."

Hey, no fair! There's no such thing as the Answer Fairy!
Women do process the information, but with such speed
that it defies point-by-point reasoning. Plus, they can use
their right hemisphere more than we guys, which will generate an answer without leaving a logical (left-brained) trail
to explain how they got there.

Males, however, aren't totally brain-dead. In fact, our
one-side-at-a-time tendency can work to our advantage
whenever the situation calls for logical problem solving.
Most math whizzes are male, since math is a sequential, left-
brained specialty. This is especially true when a hectic atmosphere develops, such as in a crisis.

To be sure, some super female firefighters are out there,
but part of the reason I believe males predominate in that
profession is that when, say, the blazing roof is caving in on
you, your left brain needs to kick in (to logically find the best
action plan) while the right brain is suppressed (where emotions, such as panic, would originate). This is not to say that
women can't effectively use their left hemispheres as primary and suppress feelings of panic; it's just that such a job
description is made for left-brained people. In fact, during
the Gulf War, we saw many women in combat doing just
that—letting the left hemisphere overrule the right.

BOYS AND GIRLS AT CAMP

One scene that highlights boy/girl differences is when
we have the session for seven to thirteen year olds. Our

camp is laid out so that the girls are on one side of our property and the boys are on the other. Only on special occasions do we bring them together.

On those nights we get together in an open-air roofed facility—actually, it's a basketball court by day—and have line dances, square dances, and the like—all under controlled conditions. But what I notice is how the preteen boys and girls approach the social function in very different ways.

The boys by and large either run off to the pool to swim, or they sit on the low wall surrounding the floor. The girls are so crazy about square dancing that they'll dance with each other if there are no boys willing. Thus we see the female predisposition with social activities, and the boys liking physical activity such as swimming. (Of course some fear of girls is mixed in too on the part of the boys, but I believe the preferences are still exemplary of their distinct orientations.)

Another point of contact between the boys' camp and the girls' is what we call "goodie mail." It's a sort of inter-camp mail system where different campers can write friendship notes to each other. And of course that is a high point of the girls' day. But on the boys' side it is less ecstatic. In fact, the boy who receives a typically long and mushy note from a girl camper will receive his share of kidding.

The differences in how they communicate via this special mail system are interesting. The girls will write miniature novels, with poetry and the whole shebang.

The boys, in contrast, will just scribble a crude-looking note on a scrap of paper. Or they will go another route in communicating, such as sending a messenger instead of writing.

When boys and girls get a bit older and start to think about dating, things change a bit. Girls in the early years of adolescence are more prone to having crushes on boys, and they openly share their feelings, especially with their girlfriends. Some boys may have crushes, but they aren't as free about revealing their feelings.

I have found that at about age fifteen boys start openly courting girls, with victory clearly in their sights. They want to impress girls, and they go for it, with a date as the prize. Girls on the other hand, tend to daydream about the ideal relationship with the ideal boy and are more covert in their style than the boys.

When parents have a girl of this age, they should approach discussions of relationships with boys from a feelings orientation, yet keep in mind that much idealization is going on. Help her see that she has to deal in fact and not feelings, as well as be realistic. Just because Tom smiled at her today in the hall as she walked past doesn't mean he is dreaming about her all day long.

"You Hurt My Feelings"

I have also noticed a difference in how boys and girls (and even men and women) handle hurts and other interpersonal conflicts. Boys tend to blow up quickly when angry, then cool down quickly, much like a summertime cloudburst. Girls, on the other hand, tend to remember for a long time how someone wronged them or hurt them. They can remember every word, every bit of body language at the time of the infraction, every bit of the social setting in which it happened. Their remembrance pattern more closely resembles a long, sustained winter drizzle. Since relationships are important to girls—and since their brains are wired up differently from boys—they tend to have the memory of an elephant when it comes to hurts.

We need to keep that in mind when we want to communicate with them after they've been hurt by us. The Bible's advice not to "let the sun go down while you are still angry" (Ephesians 4:26) is all the more important.

DIFFERENT DOESN'T MEAN BETTER OR WORSE

Perhaps nowhere else do we see the highly charged political atmosphere (as one researcher called it) come to the fore than in the male/female realm. In other words, some folks get highly upset whenever male/female differences are discussed. I think that is usually due to misunderstanding regarding what is meant by "different"—they think that this term necessarily implies that one gender is better than the other.

But that is not my meaning. In the beginning, God created us as different genders *on purpose,* with oneness in a marriage relationship as one of His primary purposes in bestowing such diversity (Genesis 2:18, 24). During our youth (and here's the significance for parents), we need to be nurtured in male- and female-appropriate ways, so that we can grow up to be the type of male or female God intends for us to become.

But in a sense, we're incomplete without opposite-sex relationships. We're one part of a puzzle looking for that complementary other puzzle piece, which is usually found in a marriage partner. So even though we're very different from the opposite gender, that difference is OK because it's part of the Creator's master plan. It is beautiful to see how in a marriage relationship—or in a family setting—the strengths and weaknesses of each sex can complement each other.

BEWARE PINK AND BLUE BLANKETS

See why God created two genders—and why we need each other? Don't fall into the trap of stereotyping your children by whether they came home from the hospital in blue or pink. There are few "blanket" statements that we can make about gender differences.

Remember that a full one-fifth of males do not have predominantly one-side-of-the-brain thinking. Many girls are as aggressive as the stereotypical boy. And much of what constitutes male and female behavior and roles is largely a product of our unique cultural setting.

So don't cage in your children. There are general principles that fit most children, but remember you're raising unique, one-of-a-kind kids who carry in their souls a portion of the image of God. And that diversity was intended from the beginning.

In the next two chapters we shall delve into the world of communication, covering both the verbal and nonverbal aspects. As incredible as it may sound, much more is communicated to our kids in the nonverbal realm than in the verbal. So we'll begin with the nonverbal side.

If your family seems to be lacking in the communication process (and whose isn't?), you may be amazed to find out what kind of things are being communicated without words.

Notes

1. James Watkins, *Sex Is Not a Four-Letter Word* (Wheaton: Tyndale, 1991), p. 182.
2. Norman Geschwind, "Proceedings of the National Academy of Sciences," *USA '79*, 1982, pp. 5097-100.
3. Janice T. Gibson, "Are Boys and Girls Really So Different?" *Parents* (September 1990): 157.
4. "Profile: Viva La Difference—Doreen Kimura Plumbs Male and Female Brains," *Scientific American* (October 1990): 42.

Thinking It Over

1. Besides the obvious external differences in male and female infants, what other differences do you sense?
2. What are some gender-based characteristics you have noticed while you have attended an athletic event? Keep this question in mind the next time you attend a competition.
3. List and discuss conversational differences in the sexes. What significance do you find in these differences?
4. What can you do to better develop your listening skills, especially with regard to relating best to the males and females in your family?
5. What was the most significant thing you learned from this chapter concerning male/female differences? How can you apply that to your relationship with your spouse and opposite-sex children?

CHAPTER TEN

The Incredible Power of Nonverbal Communication

S uzette grew up a debutante in Little Rock, Arkansas, in an upper middle-class family with, as we say in Arkansas, "all the fixins."

On the other hand, I grew up on poke salad. (For those of you who didn't grow up in the South, poke salad is a "delicacy" made up of greens picked on a walk through the woods. It may taste a bit gamey, but the price is right!) Suffice to say that we grew up on different sides of the tracks.

But Suzette continues to try to civilize me. For instance, she insists that each member of our family puts his napkin on his lap when we sit down to dinner.

Since I've never understood why anyone would want a greasy napkin on his lap, I started secretly slipping it under the tablecloth. *There*, I thought, *I'm keeping Suzette happy and my jeans clean.*

That is, until Suzette caught the children with *their* napkins stuffed under the tablecloth. "Where did you learn to do that?" she demanded. Three pairs of eyes stared in my direction. Then Suzette glared at me. "What a fine example you are, Jim!" I was caught dead in her sights.

Modeling is never an option for parents; it's a fact. Our kids are watching our behavior and are soaking it up like sponges. We are models—for good or for bad.

IT'S WHAT YOU DON'T SAY THAT COUNTS

In the next chapter we'll talk about verbal communication. But for now we'll discover how nonverbal messages communicate our values and beliefs more strongly than our actual words do.

For instance, I can tell our dog, with my lips, "Josie, you are the ugliest excuse for a flea-bitten, tick-infected, worm-ridden, runny-eyed mutt I've ever seen." But if I say that with a big smile and pleasant tone while gently petting her, she'll wag her tail with glee because I've communicated something entirely contrary to the meaning of my words.

And it works just as well in reverse. I can tell Josie how much I love her, but if I do it with a scowl while shaking a stick at her, I communicate anger and hatred rather than affection.

It works the same with humans. Researchers tell us that less than 10 percent of human communication is with actual words. Fully one-third is communicated by tone of voice and more than half by body language.

That's why, I believe, God commanded the Israelites:

Love the Lord your God with all your heart and with all your soul and with all your strength. These commandments that I give you today are to be upon your hearts. Impress them on your children. Talk about them when you sit at home and when you walk along the road, when you lie down and when you get up. (Deuteronomy 6:5-7)

Notice that the word *talk* is used only once. We are not told to love God with our mouths but with heart, soul, and strength. Therefore our actions should reflect Christ and be a natural part of every moment of our day. St. Francis of Assisi once stated, "Proclaim Christ in everything you do. If necessary, use words."

SPRAY PAINTING MODELS

In this way, values and beliefs are more "caught" than "taught." Pastor and author Jim Watkins illustrates parenting with the following story. He and his five-year-old son Paul decided one weekend to repaint Paul's bike. They spent hours sanding down chipped areas on the fenders and cleaning the chrome sprockets and handlebars.

All the while, Paul was getting more and more impatient. "Come on, Dad. When are we going to paint it?"

Finally by Saturday afternoon the time had arrived to paint the bike with gray primer.

"Why do we have to do that?" Paul demanded. "Let's just paint it jet black."

"Well, that helps the outside paint to stick on better," Jim tried to explain as he shook the can of spray paint.

"Can I do it, Dad? I'll be careful," Paul said. Jim decided to let his little son have a try at it.

Jim thought he had explained the fine art of spray painting to Paul. But once the can of paint was in Paul's hand, he aimed it at the back fender and bombarded one small area. Quickly the thick paint began running in little gray rivulets over the edge of the fender.

"Remember, Paul, you've got to use real thin coats of paint."

"But it doesn't cover anything that way," countered his son.

"Well, it takes lot of thin coats. Sometimes the coats don't even show up. But if you just keep putting on thin coat after thin coat, pretty soon it begins to show." Jim demonstrated as Paul watched in amazement. "Here, now you try it."

Watkins reminds us, "Parenting is like that. If we bombard our children with lectures, the values we want to teach often 'run'—or worse, our children 'run' from us. But it's the many thin coats of advice—backed up by our actions—that begin to slowly build up and produce a high gloss finish in our children's lives."[1]

PAINTING VALUES AND BELIEFS

Suzette and I have tried to "spray" three things onto our children through verbal as well as nonverbal communication. They go in this order.

First is the importance of God. I view my kids as my primary disciples, since they are my investment in the future for the cause of Christ. What I want my kids to say most about me is, "My dad loved God more than anything in the world." I want them to see this lived out through my actions, my attitudes, my relationships, and my priorities.

I often tell my kids that they're a gift from God to me. And if they can see that, they can't help but notice how much I love their mom and them. That's because authentic love permeates a home.

Second is the importance of one's spouse. Someone has said that one of the most important things a dad can do for his kids is to love their mom. I want my tone of voice and body language to convince my kids that I love and cherish Suzette above all others.

Third is the importance of our children. Since more than one-half of our daily communication is transmitted through body language, I want every part of me to communicate that importance. Let's go back to the incident when Jill interrupted the work I was doing on this book, as explained earlier.

When she brought me her "spin art" project, my smile told her, "It's OK to show me your art even though I'm busy." If I had frowned, rolled my eyes in frustration, crossed my arms, slumped my shoulders, or not made eye contact, my actions would have told her silently (but very specifically): "Get lost. I'm busy!" She would have heard loud and clear that she wasn't valuable in my economy.

My friends Gary Smalley and John Trent tell the story of the wife who was frustrated with her husband's "angry and dishonoring" body language. Inspired by the hidden camera shows on TV, she mounted a small camcorder in a bookshelf and turned it on as soon as she heard her husband's car pull up.

During the evening the wife brought up her concern about her husband's angry body language. As he was denying such a thing, she revealed the camera and put the tape in the VCR. The husband was stunned as he watched how many times he had rolled his eyes back, crossed his arms, and refused to make eye contact with his wife. All he could say was, "Is that really me? Do I really look that way?"[2]

A family version of "Candid Camera" might be an education for all in your family as well.

Meaningful touches—pats on the back, friendly punches in the arm, hugs, firm handshakes, and so on—are an important and essential way to show others how important they are. Several medical studies have shown that those who receive four or more healthy hugs a day actually have longer life expectancy. In fact, one study revealed that babies who were not held as infants actually died from lack of physical contact—even though all their other physical needs were fulfilled. Make sure your children aren't dying for healthy physical affection.

I would sound two cautions as your children become teenagers. First, don't stop hugging. Many fathers stop hugging their developing daughters just when they need healthy hugging the most. If they're not getting the "minimum daily requirement" of meaningful touches at home, they'll turn to the world for physical affirmation.

Second, be sensitive of their feelings. As children go through puberty, they begin to feel more modest and protective of their bodies. Suzette is the very best at maintaining an open, honest communication with our kids about sex, their bodies, and such. She'll ask, "Are you uncomfortable about sitting in my lap or our hugging and kissing?"

Fortunately, hugging and kissing has been something our children have grown up with and continue to feel free to express themselves in healthy physical affection. I am sensitive, however, when we're in public such as at the airport when the kids are meeting me. I let them, particularly sixteen-year-old Jason, initiate hugs.

The important thing is to keep the channels of communication open. (We'll talk about that in the next chapter.)

There are thousands of ways that we communicate how important our children are.

When Jason was six years old, he volunteered to help paint the house. The logical part of me knew that he'd get more paint on the driveway and himself than on the house. But I knew I wanted him to feel important, so I forced myself to hand over the paint brush to Jason.

At dinner—after we had spent an hour cleaning up—Jason proudly announced, "Hey, Mom, I helped Dad paint the house!" Then he turned to me, "Daddy, can I help you paint tomorrow?" Even though the perfectionist inside me was screaming no, I wanted Jason to know that I love him more than I love perfection. So I said yes.

Another way to communicate value is merely having my warm body sitting in the audience of a school play or on the bleacher at the soccer field. My mere presence shouts, "What you're doing at school is important to me. *You* are important to me."

Suzette and I have also taken a more active role in their lives. For instance, I recently ran for our local school board (I lost, but it was a good learning experience—maybe I'll win next time). Involvement in your kid's world pays rich dividends.

When Suzette quit her job to open a gymnastics class so she could spend more time with Jason and Travis, that communicated: "You're more important than a new car or a job with good benefits."

George Loss was a real winner when it came to affirming the players on the team. As I worked for George as an inner-city coach, I noticed how he handled interruptions during staff meetings. Instead of telling a player, "Can't you see we're busy?" George stopped whatever we were discussing to hear out his player. No wonder the kids loved George—and knew that he loved them.

SPRAY PAINT AND OTHER ADULTS

Being a single parent is a challenge because there is only one parent to provide moral and emotional support in the draining responsibility of raising children.

And the child is left without a role model of the sex opposite to the remaining parent. Married couples can in fact be single parents as well. Some parents simply refuse to take on their parenting responsibilities and thus remain disengaged—even though they are physically in the home. As you'll see in the next chapter, I unconsciously allowed my work to make me an absent parent for a time.

Perhaps the spouse is addicted to work or alcohol and is not in the home when he or she is needed by the children. A serious hospitalization can cause a spouse temporarily to become a single parent. In the case of a remarriage, a child may not accept the new parent, so the original parent is often forced to assume the single parent role.

In the case of the single parent and the functionally single parent, choose a role model of the same sex as the missing spouse. The most important requirement is that the role model share your moral, ethical, and spiritual values. A brother/sister, aunt/uncle, godparent, or friend at church can help fill the gap. Invite that person to go with you to school activities and church events. Have him—or her—baby-sit your children.

Other model families are as important to the two-parent family as to the single-parent family. Suzette and I actively search out and find families that are admirable in our church or community. This also helps fill in the personality gaps in a family. Since there are no strong Beavers in our household, we try to associate with Beaver families in order that they can model organization to our fly-by-the-seat-of-the-pants family.

We also expose our children to Christian sports models. John Brandis, tight end for the Indianapolis Colts, serves as a counselor at our camps. So one weekend, Travis and I traveled to Indianapolis, stayed with my brother, and then watched John play in the Hoosier Dome.

That's not to say that we travel around the country following sports stars. Jason admires John Nabors, an Olympic gold medal backstroker. The closest we've ever got to this athlete is the ESPN channel, but it is still a good influence to hear John make open remarks about his faith on national television.

You can provide superstar models through books, articles, videos, or by writing a fan letter. You'll be surprised how many of them actually write back. I would caution parents—and their children—not to put their faith in the superstars of music and sports, however. Stress the role model's faith in Christ, not an unrealistic view of his humanity.

Spray Paint and Peers

Older children are powerful models—for both good and bad—for younger children. In my experience as a teacher and principal, I've seen this happen over and over. It can sometimes be a motivator for older kids to live right, since the younger kids are watching them and learning from them. It is also a boost to an older child's self-esteem to realize that younger kids are looking up to her.

But the wrong peers can be dangerous. Suzette and I have tried to provide our kids with good peer models during the grade school years before they reach puberty, when loyalty and allegiance shifts from parents to peers.

We've made it a point to meet the parents of our children's friends by inviting them to dinner, cookouts, or to ride to out-of-town games with us. We also let our kids invite their friends over for an evening of fun activities or even a canoeing trip. This way there is two-way modeling going on.

Our family tries to model a healthy balanced family lifestyle, and the "invitees" are hopefully modeling a healthy balanced lifestyle to our children in return.

We also want to make life in our home so inviting that the hearts of both our kids and their friends will be attracted to us, rather than to the wrong crowd at school. For instance, Jason has a friend who loves to hang around at our house. The friend's family has a lot of violence in it, and he is amazed that we don't shout and throw things at each other. We're not perfect, but we're working on the quality of our family life—and the quality of other families'.

Remember that although you are the most powerful model in your child's life, you should avoid pressuring your children to follow exactly in your footsteps. Not only can that squash individuality and blur their unique identity, but it can lead to performance-based acceptance.

Jim Watkins sums up his SPRAY PAINT talk with a drawing that graphically reveals how we can T-A-M-E our family zoo:

How to T-A-M-E Your Family Zoo

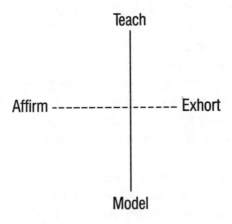

Teach

Affirm ---------------|-------- Exhort

Model

Think of these four points as the four legs on a table. For there to be ''balance'' in the home, what we *Teach* must be consistent with what we *Model*.

Note that the horizontal scale is weighted to the left, toward *Affirmation*. This is not a typo! It's because our *Exhortation* (correction) of our children must be balanced with *Affirmation*.

Because negative words weigh more heavily on us all, there needs to be much more praise than constructive criticism to stay in balance.

For example, just because you were a Boy Scout doesn't mean your son has to join up. If he does, however, that doesn't mean he has to earn an Eagle Scout rank just because you did. If you took ballet lessons, that doesn't mean your daughter wants to become a prima ballerina.

Allow each child to explore his own interests, then support him not only with your words but also with your actions.

Though the importance of nonverbal communication is staggering, the verbal side is all-important too. In the next chapter we'll explore three secrets to effective verbal interaction with our family members.

Whether you're blessed with having high Otter family members who talk, talk, talk, or with having Retriever members who have to be drawn out verbally, these concepts will help improve this critical area of family life.

Notes

1. Jim Watkins, in a sermon delivered at LaOtto Wesleyan Church, LaOtto, Indiana, on 11 November 1990.
2. Gary Smalley and John Trent, *The Two Sides of Love* (Pomona, Calif.: Focus on the Family, 1990), p. 126.

Thinking It Over

1. What are some significant differences between verbal and nonverbal communication? List and/or discuss ways that you have communicated nonverbally in the last couple of days.
2. Which of your children is most affected by destructive nonverbal communication? Have you experienced her closed spirit when you have used nonverbals to the extreme? How could you become more sensitive to her feelings?
3. What would a secret videotape reveal about your use of nonverbals with your family members?
4. What areas of communication could we "spray paint" onto our behavior patterns to make us more effective communicators with those we love?

CHAPTER ELEVEN

Verbal Communication: Talking to the Animals

You want to do *what*, Jason?" I tried to control the tone of my voice, but shock and disapproval were overshadowing my actual words. (My nonverbals were communicating louder than my verbals.)

"I want a 'Boz' haircut," Jason repeated with pleading eyes and a bit of a whine in his voice. (For the non–sports fans, I should explain that football star Brian Bozworth sports a haircut that only a punk-rocker could love. The top is cut in a short flat-top, the sides are shaven, and the back is left to grow long.)

As I continued objecting as gently as possible, I didn't pick up on my son's nonverbal messages. His head drooped, his eyes avoided mine, and he dragged himself off to his room with a deflated, "Yeah, OK."

I soon realized there was more to his request than just a new hairstyle. I knocked on his door.

"Come in." He sighed.

"Jason, is there something more to wanting a 'Boz' cut than just hair?"

He shrugged his shoulders. I waited.

"It's just that Brian and I agreed to both get one."

Now it began to make sense. Jason, our Golden Retriever, didn't see this as merely a haircut but as a bond between two friends. I had wrongly assumed that such a hairstyle meant my son was turning anti-establishment.

But since the motive for wanting the haircut was a relationship and not rebellion, I said, "Well, why don't you take some time to think about it before you actually head for the barber. You know you'll always have my unbounded love and acceptance—even if I personally don't approve of every action. So if, after you've really thought through the consequences, you decide to get a 'Boz' cut, you have my blessing."

After a couple hours, Jason came downstairs.

"Y'know, Dad, that was a pretty dumb idea about getting my hair cut that way, wasn't it?"

This incident points out two important principles. One, the question that our children approach us with is often not the real issue. With Jason, the haircut was only an indication of a deeper question: "Can I do something with a friend that will deepen our relationship?" (For Retrievers, the motivation or desire is usually hiding beneath the surface question.) My tone of voice and disapproving body language almost stopped communication at skin-deep level.

Second, many times our children really do want to communicate with us but are afraid of our disapproval.

I should point out that I've not always been that compassionate and understanding with my children or with Suzette. The ability to communicate is not automatic or inborn. It's a skill that is learned over time and takes a lot of practice.

Suzette and I have used three tools that have greatly helped our communication with our children and each other.

COMMUNICATION TOOLS

QUICK LISTENING

An old story tells about a young farmer who was struggling to get his mule to move. He had coaxed it with a carrot, had tried pulling and pushing, but the mule stubbornly sat in the middle of the road.

Finally an old farmer pulled up beside him with his mule and cart. The young farmer explained that he needed to get the load of hay to market, but midway to town the mule had suddenly stopped in its tracks and wouldn't budge.

The old farmer casually walked to the back of his wagon, pulled out a six-foot-long two-by-four, and clobbered the young farmer's mule right between the eyes. The mule leaped forward like lightning—and didn't stop till it reached town.

"First, son," the old farmer advised, "you've got to get the mule's attention."

Quick listening is the two-by-four between our eyes that gets our attention so we can listen effectively to our children.

One day I was hit between the eyes. Travis kept coming downstairs to the office asking me questions. I would grunt a few "uh huhs," and he would run back up to his room. Finally, after about an hour, Travis came storming downstairs, saying, "It's all your fault, Dad! I don't think you were even listening to me."

"Uh huh."

"Dad!"

"What?" I asked. Travis finally had my attention.

"You weren't listening to me when I was asking you questions. And now look what I've done." Travis hurried up to his room. "See!"

There in his bedroom was a full-sized basketball goal, board, and pole.

"I put it together like you said, and now I can't get it outside!"

Had I really said "uh huh" to putting together a full-sized, regulation basketball goal in his bedroom?

If I had just spent thirty seconds really listening to what Travis had asked an hour ago, I wouldn't have spent thirty minutes helping him get this beast out of his room.

The secret to quick listening is to give the child all your attention as you watch for nonverbal and verbal communication. That means no distractions: turn off the TV (or at least punch the "mute" button), put down the newspaper, swing around from your desk to face him, or hold him on your lap so he knows you are listening, not just with your ears but with your whole body.

Jill's best time to unload is at bedtime. I don't stand by her bed (that would communicate that I'm in a hurry), but I either kneel by her bed or lie down beside her. That way, I communicate, "You're the most important person in my life right now."

"What happened in school today, Jill?" Her silence (nonverbal message) screamed that something went wrong. "Did something happen today that upset you?"

"Well," Jill stammered, "there were some kids making fun of me because that I have to go to the [remedial] reading lab."

"How did that make you feel?" I asked.

Jill paused. She was uncomfortable expressing that feeling. So I prompted, "Are you saying that those kids made you feel dumb and stupid?"

Somberly, Jill's little head bobbed up and down. Part of quick listening is repeating back to our child what we think we heard her say. If you've got it wrong, she'll let you know, and you can try again. It helps us focus in on exactly what the child wants to communicate.

I wanted to get to a solution phase, so I gently asked, "Do you have any ideas about what we can do about it?" (We'll talk about family brainstorming in the next chapter.)

Another painful pause. Then she suggested, "Well, maybe we can go to the library more often."

Breakthrough!

I made a quick decision and said to her, "I have an appointment tomorrow, but I can cancel it so we can go together."

"All *right*, Dad!" she responded. She hugged me and snuggled under the covers. The whole conversation took less than one minute, and yet because I gave her my total attention, she was completely satisfied.

I'm not advocating simply being a one-minute father. Kids need quantity as well as quality in parental relationships. But quick listening is one way to open the lines of communication—no matter how busy we become.

One family I know tells about the time their two sons came home from spending the weekend at another family's home. The visit went well in general, but the oldest son, Jimmy, said to his mother, "Mom, I'm glad we talk a lot in our family."

The mother, a bit puzzled by such a statement alone, wanted to know what was behind it. "What do you mean, Jimmy? Didn't they allow you to talk during the weekend?"

"Oh, sure, we could talk. But what I meant was that sometimes when Mr. and Mrs. Jones were angry with us, they would just glare at us with a hateful look. And I wouldn't know *why* they were doing it. It made me scared and confused." Apparently one time Jimmy's little brother, who has a strong Otter trait, wasn't getting in the car fast enough for the high Beaver parents. (He was probably running around the car three times before getting in, just for the fun of it!) So instead of simply telling the little brother, "Please get in the car now," they glared at Jimmy.

Jimmy continued sharing his feelings with his mother "Mom, I'm glad that in our family when we're upset with another person, we just say so. That way we know where we stand and don't have to worry so much."

I can't overemphasize the importance of talking out our feelings in the family setting. Friction is a natural thing in families and is OK when handled in a straightforward and honest manner. Unexplained nonverbals such as burning glares don't help at all.

EMOTIONAL BAROMETERS

Suzette is the most balanced person I know, but the Lion in her wants to get to the point. When she would ask me, "What's wrong?" she expected a concise answer. But because I'm an Otter/Retriever, my answers tended to wander and dwell mostly on how I was feeling about the issue. This would cause her Lion blood to begin boiling until "Just give me a straight answer" would bubble out.

We've learned to ask our children, "On a scale of one to ten how do you feel about such and such?"

For instance, I needed to know how Travis felt about staying home with Jill while Suzette and I went to Jason's ball game. An eight or ten tells us, "Yeah, that would be great!" Something under four means, "That's really the last thing I'd like to do."

Emotional barometers are good for simple checks, but for more complex issues and feelings we use emotional word pictures.

EMOTIONAL WORD PICTURES[1]

Christ was an expert in using one picture to explain a thousand words. Instead of talking about hypocrisy, Christ talked about whitewashed tombs. He illustrated His desire to reach the lost with stories of lost sheep, the lost coin, and the powerful story of the lost (prodigal) son. Instead of giving a dictionary definition of "neighbor," He told the now classic story of the Good Samaritan.

Word pictures visualize what words cannot communicate. And so they have become an important part of our family communication. I really needed a way to express to Suzette how I felt when I walked in the door and was confronted with a list of family responsibilities I had neglected. We had been married for twelve years, and I had never told her my feelings.

Finally one night, after suspending three students, severely reprimanding one teacher, and losing a football game, I was met at the door with, "Why can't you help around the house. Why don't you spend time with the kids? All you do is hide away in the den watching films of next week's football opponents."

I was also met at the door by Josie, our black Labrador, with her tail wagging, showing how glad she was to see me. At that point I thought of the right word picture. I practiced it a few times with a close friend from school so I would get it right.

Then that evening when the kids were asleep and Suzette and I were in bed, I pulled her close to me.

"Honey, do you remember going coon hunting with your granddaddy?" Suzette loved her grandfather, so she was instantly on-line with me as she fondly remembered those days.

"Remember how he told us that sometimes one of the coon dogs would get lost? He would leave a blanket that had his scent on the ground. The next morning the exhausted hound, who was bruised and bloodied from finding its way back through the underbrush, would be lying on the blanket eagerly waiting for the joyful reunion with his master."

Suzette snuggled closer as I continued.

"But what if your granddaddy, instead of hugging and comforting the dog, took off his belt and beat him for getting lost. 'Bad dog!' he would shout."

Suzette stiffened in my arms at the picture of such cruelty. I took a deep breath before going on.

"Suzette, that's how I feel when I come home from a day of giving and giving and giving, and you beat me at the door with, "Why didn't you do this and that?"" There was a long, heavy silence.

"Oh, Jim," she finally sobbed, "I had no idea that's how you felt." Although I had no idea how powerful this word picture would be, the feelings it captured brought to the surface all the emotions we'd been repressing, and that really surprised us both. After two hours of tears and deep soul searching, we reached a deeper level of understanding. It was painful, but working through such a significant problem brought us together in a way that nothing else could.

But a few weeks later, I was on the receiving end of another powerful word picture.

The kids were at a sitter's, and Suzette and I were enjoying an evening at our favorite frozen yogurt shop.

"Remember those chocolate-covered strawberries you enjoy during the summer?" Suzette asked.

Remember? I could taste them! I used to stand in long lines during tourist season in Branson for those wonderful chocolate-covered strawberries.

Suzette continued. "Imagine that The Fudge Shop just made their last batch of the season."

"You bet I can," I replied enthusiastically.

"Well, imagine, Jim, that you're the last person in line waiting to make your final purchase of the season. You watch intently as each person checks out at the cash register. Your mouth is watering so badly that you have to keep swallowing to avoid drooling. Finally, you step up to the counter in eager anticipation, only to hear the clerk announce they just sold their last strawberry. How would that make you feel?"

"I'd feel cheated and totally frustrated," I quickly answered.

Now it was Suzette's turn to take a deep breath and knock the wind out of me. "That's how I feel. Every night when you come home, I'm the last person in that long, long line, Jim."

I stared in disbelief at my empty yogurt dish. "I don't understand."

"Every day it's as if you're that clerk," she began. "You give and give and give to everyone at the school, but when you come home to the kids and me you're all 'sold out.' There's nothing left for us. You escape with the newspaper or TV, and we feel cheated and frustrated because you don't have anything left for us."

Just as Suzette had no idea how I felt when I came home, for twelve years I had no idea how she felt. I didn't quit my job, but I did start looking at my day in a radically different way. I had been lulled into the world's mold of the conquering male who worked at the office, then came home to relax with his slippers and the evening paper.

I began to rearrange my priorities at the office. I delegated more work to others. I also began to realign my spiritual priorities. After what seemed to be a season of prayers, I sensed the Holy Spirit's power to help me come through a stressful day and still have strength to be with and enjoy my family. And I began to apply James 1:2-10 to my daily work load ("Consider it all joy . . . when you encounter various trials," NASB). I saw tense situations not as something to drain me but rather as things that God could use to make me a better person—and a better husband and father.

One practical thing I did was cancel the newspaper subscription and spend the time finding out my family's daily news. And I found myself more motivated to help Suzette around the house. As a result I became a better model of how a man should love his wife and family.

Suzette and I have used this same method with our children. For instance, one day Jason—who was on the verge of driver's education—said, "I feel like a '57 Chevy." So I played along and asked, "What condition is the car in? Has it got bright, shiny paint and mint-condition interior? Or is the paint scratched up and the taillights kicked out?"

"Well, I feel like I've been rear-ended," Jason answered. "I feel like all weekend long all I've gotten from you is negative feedback. You been kicking my tail all weekend, and I feel pretty emotionally banged up."

Again I felt like I had been broadsided. I guess I had been kidding him a lot that weekend. What I thought was good-natured humor had been cruel put-downs to my son. Once I was made aware of that, we were able to work through our misunderstanding.

Use what your child really enjoys in your word picture. If your child loves stuffed animals, ask, "Which one of your animals do you feel most like?" Then ask why. You'll discover that they feel like the droopy-eyed puppy because they're sad about something that happened at school. Or they may pick a funny clown because that's how they feel.

If your children are taking music lessons, ask, "What kind of music do you feel like today? Rock, jazz, gospel, rap, or a funeral dirge?"

Some readers may think that emotional word pictures are simply a way to manipulate others—find a person's most sensitive nerve, open it up, and pour acid on it. Please understand, the purpose is not to scald the other person but to let him see something important in the relationship. It's "speaking the truth in love" (Ephesians 4:15).

The most important thing is to listen with open body language and open acceptance.

We've covered a lot of ground so far, and now we're ready for the last stop in our tour of how to strengthen family connections. Understanding personality types is extremely helpful, but it's only a good foundation for improving family life.

Comprehending personality mix is an essential road map for enhancing family relationships, but there comes a phase in implementing these concepts when you have to blend that understanding together with healthy portions of love, respect, and family loyalty. Our last chapter covers such ingredients.

Note

1. This concept was popularized by John Trent and Gary Smalley in *The Language of Love* (Pomona, Calif.: Focus on the Family, 1988). If you would like to know more about emotional word pictures, I suggest you read that book.

Thinking It Over

1. Why does "just saying no" to your child elicit a chorus of, "Why?" How does a child's response differ with personality types?
2. How can you best keep open lines of communication with your teenager when he tells you something that shocks you?
3. What conditions exist in your home (or heart) that hinder you from being capable of "quick listening"? Try this technique and share its benefits with a friend or fellow parent this week.
4. When is the best time for your child to communicate to you how his day went?
5. What are some of your children's favorite toys, games, cars, and so on? With this in mind, make up an emotional word picture that would motivate them to help around the house, settle a conflict, or let them know how you feel about them. Try it out on the children, then discuss the results with your spouse.

CHAPTER TWELVE

Turning a Jungle into a Game Preserve

I had blown it with Jason. But I wasn't ready to admit it—at least then. So instead of Jason's taking the bus to school, I decided to drive him.

We both avoided eye contact as we drove along in silence—until we were about three or four minutes from school. It was now or never.

"Jason, I was wrong. I shouldn't have gotten all over your case when you were running late getting ready for school. Maybe having you get up earlier than Travis is the solution, but we can talk about that later. It's just that I don't want you to carry this inside the school doors with you today, so I'm admitting that I was wrong. Would you please forgive me?"

"Yeah, Dad, I will," Jason said, as our eyes finally connected.

I gratefully replied, "I know we don't have time to talk about it, but tonight we'll talk it over."

"That'd be great, Dad," Jason replied with a big smile.

I felt much better that our relationship had been restored before I turned him out into that deep, dark jungle. He now could go through the day looking forward to getting back to the Brawner game preserve, rather than trying to find comfort and acceptance in a hostile world.

Some of the tragic trends we discussed in chapter 1 could be avoided if parents would make their home a loving refuge where children could receive the emotional strength and affirmation they need to make it through the tough days. One popular song sung by country singer Ronnie Milsap extols a daddy's love for his wife, especially regarding this idea of refuge:

> She keeps the home fires burning.
> While I'm out earning a living in a world
> that's known for its pouring rain.
>
> She keeps the home fires burning.
> And it's her warm loving
> that keeps me returning again . . . and again.[1]

Our world really can be full of pouring rain, and the hotter we stoke the home fires, the more our family members are going to be attracted to and draw their support from the home's hearth. Then our kids will have the strength to resist peer pressure and be able to walk more confidently through life's travails. With a strong family background in their hip pocket, they'll be prepared for practically anything this world can throw at them.

THE ZOO REVIEW: FAMILY DECISION MAKING

One way that we have tried to cultivate an environment where it is safe to express oneself is by family goal-setting meetings. We don't schedule them; they're spontaneous—held on Mom and Dad's king-sized bed or around the dinner table. They're called when we need to plan a family vacation or party, settle a conflict, or develop a discipline policy.

We use the acrostic G-O-A-L-S as a kind of agenda at each meeting.

Say for instance that we want a new car. The first stage is G for "gather." We gather as many ideas as possible. At this point it's all "green light thinking." No idea, no matter what, is criticized as we talk. Sometimes we write our ideas down on three-by-five cards, and at other times just call them out and write them down on a chalkboard.

"I want a customized van."

"I want a Lambourghini!"

"I want a mini-van."

"I want a Porsche!"

"How about a Jeep to go camping with?"

"Or maybe a pickup with a camper."

Everyone—no matter how young—has a chance to express his or her thoughts and desires. Otters have the most fun with this stage, so tap into their creativity. Lions, however, are wanting to move on to the bottom line, so try to hold them back if necessary to complete the whole process.

The next step is O for "organize." We begin to categorize our ideas. This is where the Beavers can use their gifts to the fullest, since they are masters of organization.

"Let's see, these break down into categories of vans, Jeeps, and sports cars."

Notice that no one is allowed to say, "That's a dumb idea," in these first two stages. Only at the third stage (the letter A in the acrostic) does our family begin to "analyze" how practical the ideas are. The Golden Retriever is especially good here, since he takes each member into consideration.

"I don't think a sports car or a pickup truck would work for a family of five." Notice that the idea is what is being analyzed, not the person who came up with the idea. "And be-sides, we don't have the money for a Porsche."

L is for "limit." Our family crosses off ideas that are be-yond our financial or time resources. When we went through this process with Jason's car, the prices ranged be-tween $150 and $19,000! After adding up his savings ac-count, his odd jobs, the money that Jill and Travis offered to kick in (for rides to school with big brother), and the half that Suzette and I offered to pay, Jason had a good idea of what he could spend on a car. Needless to say, the Lam-bourghini lost out.

You'll also need to cross off ideas that someone in the family just couldn't live with.

"I would be embarrassed to go to school in a pickup truck with a camper."

Lions love the bottom line mentality of this limiting phase. This whole process helps each personality to see the importance of each step. Otters tend to be great idea people but often lack follow through. Beavers aren't always creative in the gathering stage but shine in the organizing phase. And Golden Retrievers' desire for harmony keeps the whole process from degenerating into thermonuclear family war.

Finally, after a decision is made, we move to S for "start." We started looking through newspaper ads, check-ing out the dealerships, talking to friends, neighbors, and a trusted mechanic. Unless something is started after the dis-cussion, the process is simply dreaming and really not goal setting or decision making.

As I mentioned earlier, these G-O-A-L-S sessions can also be an effective way of handling major discipline issues or even resolving conflicts.

Rod and Vicki Pock have used this tool with their two sons, Justin and Ryan.

"We seem to have a conflict over who watches what programs on TV? Let's do some 'green light thinking,' kids," Rod suggested.

"You and Mom could buy us each a TV for our own rooms." (Rod had to force himself not to throw up a barricade at that "green light" suggestion.)

"Maybe we could watch some shows live while videotaping a show that somebody else wants to watch," Ryan added.

"Maybe we could make a list of our three favorite programs and then we could make a chart to make sure that we get to watch our very favorites," Vicki said. (Can you guess what kind of personality type would make that suggestion?)

"How about the one who does the dishes that night gets first pick of what shows we watch?" (This child wants to have credit where credit is due!)

After Gathering ideas, the Pocks Organized them, Analyzed them for practicality, Limited them (the family budget just didn't allow three TVs), and then they Started in.

Write Out Your Parenting Goals

Since goals that are never written down are simply wishes, Suzette and I have written some specific goals for us parents. She keeps it beside our bed as a constant reminder.

Our list isn't sacred. You and your spouse can formulate your own parenting goals and keep them handy. For the sake of illustration, here is our list:

Things I Want My Children to Master Before They Leave Home

1. Love and honor God
2. Respect others' feelings
3. Respect others' property
4. Respect authority
5. Take care of your own belongings
6. Learn the value of money
7. Learn the value of time
8. Have healthy self-esteem

9. Take care of your body
10. Respect elders
11. Use common courtesy (e.g., social skills such as using good manners, shaking hands, saying thank you, and so on)
12. Have good table manners and practice basic etiquette
13. Give time to church and community
14. Learn to win and lose gracefully
15. Develop humility
16. Learn to really listen to and value other people

Using this kind of family decision-making and goal-setting process not only teaches good management skills but helps promote some of the qualities that we have listed as our parenting goals. Let me briefly elaborate on some of the key elements.

COMMUNICATIONS

"Green light" brainstorming allows each member to express himself in a sheltered environment free from criticism. Remember, there are no dumb or stupid ideas at this stage (or at any other)—only ones that are within or beyond our "limits."

We even used the G-O-A-L-S system when building our house. I handed out a piece of paper to each member and said, "OK, kids, pretend that's a thirty-by-forty-foot box with two floors. What are we going to put in it?" Jason and Travis wanted a weight and exercise room. Jill wanted a hot tub and a huge closet in her room. Suzette wanted each part of the house to be open so you could communicate wherever you happened to be.

It was a time of bonding as we tackled the job of designing our house and then subcontracting the work out. Today it's "our" house, which brings me to another result of family decision making.

LOYALTY

Our kids love having their friends come over to "their" house. I'm sure that some of the reason is they have had ownership in its design.

But ownership also includes the rules and regulations of a home as well. I was made aware of that by my high school football coach. He established a discipline committee of three players who decided whether someone who broke training rules would just run laps or be kicked off the team. He wanted us to own our disciplinary policy.

The coach was a believer in the K-I-S-S principle (Keep It Simple, Silly). He never resorted to anything fancy in terms of game strategy, but he instilled an incredible loyalty to the team in us. We owned our team, our discipline, and our training. As a result, we went from a 0-win, 12-loss season to winning all but one game in the season of my senior year. And our coach has succeeded, too. Today he's a coach for the Tampa Bay Buccaneers.

If your family team feels that they have had a say in the outing, discipline, or conflict resolution, they will be more likely to support it. Plus they'll grow in the process.

RESPECT

Respect can't be demanded; it must be earned and modeled by who we are and what we stand for. Through this process, children learn that their ideas are important and respected by adults. And since respect is always a two-way street, children in turn respect their parents when they feel as if they are part of the family decisions.

THE THREE RS

I trust that through our time together, you have discovered the basics that the Brawner family zoo tries to live by: R-*ules without* R-*elationship produces* R-*ebellion.*

A study several years ago tried to determine if lenient or restrictive parents produced the healthiest kids. They examined families of military men, where all was spit-and-polish. Then they examined very laissez-faire families, where there was hardly any structure at all.

What they discovered was that those kinds of environmental variables made no significant difference. Kids turned out great in both environments as long as a key element was in place: love and acceptance. High quality relationships are the key to family success.

Sometimes the tendency after reading a book on personality types is to think, *Well, I'm just a Lion, so I really can't help but growl and snarl at the kids.* But don't give up on yourself. Don't think you can't change and improve. God desires this for all of us. He calls it *sanctification.* We need to become more like Christ, who had all the personality strengths possible—and no weaknesses! He was never out of balance and always knew what trait to use when.

Over the years, our Lion Travis has become more sensitive and has developed some true Golden Retriever qualities. And this Otter dad has even developed some Beaver traits, especially while working on this book. Double-strength-Otter Jill has learned to be more Beaverlike. The secret is to try to cultivate the areas that are weak or even lacking, while continually working on open and honest relationships.

Second, don't give up on your children. Again it's tempting to think, *My kids are nearly grown. There's not really much chance of influencing them now.* But you can!

Take Tony, for example. His parents were out-of-balance Retrievers who let him grow up with few rules or restrictions. By the time Tony reached high school, his parents knew he was dealing drugs. But Tony's parents never had the courage to intervene. They would half-heartedly say, "Well, OK, we'll let it go this time, but I don't want you selling anymore."

"OK, Dad, I won't do it again," Tony would promise —with his fingers crossed.

But after sixteen years of his parents slapping his hand for wrongs, the police department put its foot down and had Tony placed in the Shelterwood youth home. Finally, Tony began receiving the tough love he had needed. The counselors were kind and polite but also firm. They did exactly what they promised to do if Tony didn't abide by the rules.

The next time I saw Tony I couldn't believe my eyes. Here was a polite, respectful young man who called me "Mr. Brawner" and said, "Yes, sir," and, "No, sir."

The Shelterwood counselors also worked with Tony's parents to show them how loving-but-firm and consistent treatment can turn even sixteen-year-old drug dealers around. Rehabilitation, however, is much more costly (in human as well as economic terms) than is doing it right the first time. And it's principles like those I present in this book that can make the difference for thousands of kids—kids like yours and mine. And for us parents, too.

LOVE CURES ALL ILLS

Bill Cosby has become America's best-known dad, given his position (in the national consciousness, anyway) as Dr. Huxtable on his TV show. In his best-selling book, *Fatherhood*, he makes some lighthearted comments that will encourage mothers as well as fathers:

> It is no profound revelation to say that fathering has changed greatly from the days when my own father used me

for batting practice. However, the baffling behavior of children is exactly the same today as it was when Joseph's brothers peddled him to the Egyptians. And in the face of such constantly baffling behavior, many men have wondered: Just what is a father's role today? . . . .

The answer, of course, is that no matter how hopeless or copeless a father may be, his role is simply to *be* there, sharing all the chores with his wife. Let her *have* the babies; but after that, try to share every job around. Any man today who returns from work, sinks into a chair, and calls for his pipe is a man with appetite for danger. Actually, changing a diaper takes much less time than waxing a car. A car doesn't spit on your pants, of course, but a baby's book value is considerably higher.

If the new American father feels bewildered and even defeated, let him take comfort from the fact that whatever he does in any fathering situation has a fifty percent chance of being right. Having five children has taught me a truth as cosmic as any that you can find on a mountain in Tibet: There are no absolutes in raising children. In any stressful situation, fathering is always a roll of the dice. The game may be messy, but I have never found one with more rewards and joys.

You know the only people who are *always* sure about the proper way to raise children? Those who've never had any.[2]

WELCOME TO THE CLUB

As we near the close of this book, I'm concerned about any readers who may be feeling bound by a suffocating and entrapping feeling of pervasive guilt. You know you've blown it many times with your kids, and you're starting to feel overwhelmed with the responsibility of it all.

But I want to underline the fact that the concepts in this book are not meant to condemn you; they're meant to help you—to help you understand yourself and the makeup of your kids. Sometimes that's half the battle!

And if you think you have blown it in parenting, welcome to the club. None of us is perfect, not even authors of parenting books.

There are two things to keep in mind as we behold this awesome task of raising our kids in the manner God wants us to:

1. Love covers a multitude of sins (see James 5:20).
2. Never give up.

In other words, remember that if you spread enough love around your home, your mistakes will pale in the light of your love. First John 4:18 says, "Perfect love casts out fear." No matter how many minor mistakes you may make, if you love your kids enough, they'll turn out a lot better than if you don't try to connect with them.

As we've seen in this book, love means listening intently to our children, making them a priority in our lives, and valuing their unique personality makeup. It means trashing the one-size-fits-all parenting method and adapting our approach to each unique child. As you implement some of the suggestions in this book, you'll be able to make that vital relational connection that will put you in good stead for preparing your kids to handle anything life throws their way.

And last of all, don't give up. You care about your family, and so does the Master Parent. He'll help you rear your kids in a healthy way. I challenge you to pray and let Him know your needs in the parenting area. Successful family life really is a partnership with God, and we need all the help we can get.

If you lean on Him and hang in there, trying each day to be the best parent (and spouse) you can be, all the while flavoring your relationships with generous amounts of love, you're going to have the success you desire. May God help us all to be the best parents we can be and raise a generation to glorify Him.

Notes

1. Mike Reid, Don Pfrimmer, Dennis Morgan, "She Keeps the Home Fires Burning." Copyright © 1985 by Lodge Hall Music, Inc. c/o MBG Songs, Inc., Collins Court Music, Inc., and Tom Collins Music, Inc. All rights reserved. Used by permission.
2. Bill Cosby, *Fatherhood* (New York: Berkeley, 1986), pp. 60-61.

Thinking It Over

1. What are the advantages of including everyone in the family in the decision-making process? What decision currently faces your family that could benefit from using the G-O-A-L-S process?

2. Make your own list of things you want your children to master before they leave home. Place your list in a significant place and discuss the items with your spouse and kids.

3. Why do you think that remembering the three Rs (Rules without Relationships produce Rebellion) is so successful in strengthening the family? How does your family atmosphere measure up on this count?

4. The saying goes, "Feed your faith, and doubt will starve to death." What can you do to strengthen your own faith (and your children's faith) so that you can stand firm against the ways of the world?

APPENDIX

Other Personality Typing Systems

T-JTA

The Taylor-Johnson Temperament Analysis test contains 180 statements that respondents answer either "decidedly so," "undecided," or, "decidedly not."

Using a rather complicated scoring procedure, the results are graphed on a continuum between "composed" and "nervous," "light-hearted" and "depressive," "active-social" and "quiet," "expressive-responsive" and "inhibited," "sympathetic" and "indifferent," "objective" and "subjective," "dominant" and "submissive," "tolerant" and "hostile," as well as "self-disciplined" and "impulsive."

Dr. Kevin Leman/Birth Order

Kevin Leman's best-selling book *The Birth Order Book* attempts to explain why you are the way you are[1] by dividing people into three broad groups: firstborns, second- (or middle-) borns, and last-borns. This psychologist believes that birth order affects our personality, whom we marry, our children, our occupational choice, and even how we relate to God.

Firstborns, according to Dr. Leman, tend to be aggressive, conscientious, overorganized perfectionists. They often bite off more than they can chew because they are people pleasers.

Second- or middle-borns seem to have more people-oriented social skills. The stereotype of the overlooked and underappreciated middle child does tend to have some validity, according to Dr. Leman. They are often the peacemakers and negotiators in the family.

The last-borns tend to coddled, so their messy, "somebody will bail me out," self-centered bent is often reinforced. They are usually people-persons, with a gift to be funny, charming, and persuasive.

Like all personality researchers, Dr. Leman stresses that these are only general tendencies.

MMPI

The Minnesota Multiphasic Personality Inventory (MMPI) is a rather technical test, which is typically used by psychiatrists and psychologists in clinical situations where moderate-to-extreme dysfunction is present.

It features 566 true/false questions that attempt to predict how a certain person will act or react in a given situation. The test is viewed as quite reliable in revealing how paranoid, depressed, manic, or anxious a person might be. It even includes a "validity scale" intended to measure if a person is lying or answering questions randomly.

It is not, however, a simple test to be used and/or understood by laypeople.

The Myers-Briggs Personality Type Indicator
This system, which is fairly easily understood and commonly used by laypeople and professionals alike in understanding personality style, divides people into four ways of interacting with others and their environment.[2] The four scales place a person's style somewhere along a continuum: introvert/extrovert, sensing/intuitive, thinking/feeling, judging/perceiving.

The first scale describes where you relate best. Extroverts are not necessarily the life of the party or the classic used car salesmen. Extroverts draw their mental and emotional energy from interacting with the outside world of people or things.

Introverts are not always wallflowers or accountants. Introverts would rather spend time in their inner world of ideas and concepts. Extroverts generate the best ideas by brainstorming with others. Introverts prefer to go off by themselves and stare into space, yet they still generate great ideas.

The second scale, Sensing and Intuitive, describes how you gather information. The Sensing type enjoys perceiving with his or her five senses. They like things that can be seen, heard, felt, tasted, or smelled. The Intuitive types, however, look at possibilities, associations, and symbols. For instance, a Sensing type would see a brilliant red sunset. An Intuitive type, however, would "see" good weather tomorrow.

The third set of opposites describe how a person makes choices. A Thinking type is not necessarily emotionless, but he or she does want decisions to be "imminently logical." A Feeling type, on the other hand, is not illogical or irrational but makes decisions on the basis of personal values.

The final pair of types are Judging and Perceiving. The Judging type has already skipped over this entire section of the book because he or she is goal-oriented. The Perceiving types are still with us because they view decision making as a process and remain open to new information, insights, and experiences.

Using these four scales it's possible to come up with sixteen different personality types. David Keirsey, a clinical psychologist, has broken these types down to four general temperaments which roughly correspond to our Lion, Otter, Retriever, and Beaver model.[3]

Notes

1. Kevin Leman, *The Birth Order Book* (Old Tappan, N.J.: Revell, 1987).
2. An excellent Christian perspective of the Myers-Briggs is by LaVonne Neff, *One of a Kind* (Portland: Multnomah, 1988).
3. Ibid., p. 67.

Moody Press, a ministry of the Moody Bible Institute,
is designed for education, evangelization, and edification.
If we may assist you in knowing more about Christ
and the Christian life, please write us without obligation:
Moody Press, c/o MLM, Chicago, Illinois 60610.